# Democratic Rotation
## in the Head of State Position in Africa

Célestin Tagou

# Democratic Rotation
# in the Head of State Position in Africa

Political Transcendence and Transformation
of Ethno-regional Conflicts in Divided Societies

*Foreword by Johan Galtung*

**Bibliographical information held by the German National Library**

The German National Library has listed this book in the Deutsche Nationalbibliografie (German national bibliography); detailed bibliographic information is available online at http://dnb.d-nb.de.

1$^{st}$ edition - Göttingen: Cuvillier, 2018

## Published by the same author

**Books**

- *Démocratie rotative et Elections présidentielles en Afrique : Transcendance et transformation politique des conflits ethno-régionaux dans les sociétés plurielles, Les cas du Cameroun et de la Côte d'Ivoire*, Editions l'Harmattan, Paris 2018
- **2017:** *Démocratie Rotative, transcendance et transformation des identités ethno-régionales dans l'Etat-Nation du 21°Siècle*, PUPA/Editions du Schabel, Yaoundé 2017
- **2016:** *Phénomène Boko Haram: Problématique de paix et sécurité au Cameroun face aux méga-conflits*, AJPCD/PUPA/ Yaoundé, 2016, Editor
- **2011:** Gestion des conflits en Afrique: Regards Croisés des jeunes chercheurs de l'UPAC, AJPCD/PUPA Yaoundé, 2011, Editor
- **2010:** *The Dynamics of Conflict, Peace and Development in African Societies*, PUPA/AIPCD Yaoundé, 2010, Editor
- **2010:** *Transcendance et Transformation des Conflits: Une Introduction au métier de Médiateur*, PUPA, Yaoundé 2010 (Traduction de Johan Galtung de l'anglais au Français)
- **2006:** *Demokratisches Rotationsprinzip: Eine Lösung für politische Integration in Kamerun*, Cuvilier Verlag, Göttingen, Germany, 2006


**Articles:**

- **2018:** « Zurück in Africa: Vom Reintegrant zum Dekant » in: Welt-Sichten, Berlin April 2018 **2017:** « Gouvernance démocratique dans un contexte pluriel » in: Simo David DAW 2017
- **2014:** « Les migrations intra africaines et leurs impacts sur la problématique de la paix et du développement en Afrique » in: Simo, David: Problématiques migratoires en contexte de globalisation, Une publication du Centre DAW de Yaoundé en collaboration avec le Goethe Institut, Yaoundé, 2014. pp.159-184
- **2013:** "Managing ethno-regional diversities in African states: Western peace paradigms versus African peace philosophy and a political way out", in: Mapinduzi Journal, Berlin, 2013. pp.147-160

- **2012:** « La typologie des minorités dans des sociétés plurielles » in: Gwoda Adder & al (sd) L'Harmattan, Paris, 2012 pp.35-49

- **2011:** « Les limites du Power Sharing dans la gestion des conflits politiques et ethno régionaux en Afrique: Le cas de la Côte d'Ivoire » in ISBN: 978-995-647-04-7 pp.11-38
- **2011:** "The relationship between universities and peace work: The case of the Faculty of Social Sciences and International Relations at the Protestant University of Central Africa", in: Kayser, Christiane&al.: Working for sustainable Peace in Cameroon, Copyright CPS/EED, Berlin, November 2011 pp.38-48
- **2011:** « Rétrospective des théories et politiques globales de développement: De Truman aux OMD » in: Pondi, Jean Emmanuel: Repenser le Développement à partir de l'Afrique, Afredit, Maisonneuve Yaounde/Paris 2011, pp.23-50
- **2010:** « Paradigmes dominants dans l'histoire de la pensée de paix: de l'universalisme antique à l'idéalisme onusien » in: PUPA/AIPCD Yaoundé, 2010, pp.29-62

# CONTENT


**DEDICATION** ....................................................................... 11

**ACKNOWLEDGEMENTS** ................................................ 13

**FOREWORD** ...................................................................... 15

**INTRODUCTION** .............................................................. 17

**CHAPTER 1** ........................................................................ 26

**Key Concepts and connotation in the 21st Century** ........... 26

  Ethnic Group and Ethnicity ......... ............................26

  The Advent of the Terms in Social Sciences and Politics ......... .........27

  What is an Ethnic Group? ........ ............................33

    *The Essentialist Approach* ................................................ 35

    *The Constructivist Approach* ........................................... 38

    *Debates with Respect to Africa* ...................................... 44

  Related Concepts: Race, Clan/Tribe, Community and People........... ...45

    *Ethnic Group and Race* ..................................................... 45

    *Ethnicity and Clan/Tribe* .................................................. 48

  The Need for a Conceptual Re-adjustment in the 21st Century .......... ...52

  What is a Nation in the 21st Century?........... ...............................53

    *The Objective Approach* ..................................................... 54

    *The Subjective Approach* .................................................... 55

  Ethnicity and the Nation: two Operational Concepts........ ...............59

**CHAPTER 2** ........................................................................ 65

**Transcendence and Transformation of
Ethno-regional Conflicts** ................................................ 65

  The New Democratic Orthodoxy ......... ............................66

  The Mismatch of the Western Model to Divided Societies .......... ......68

  Power Sharing .......... ............................74

*Power Sharing Approaches* ................................................................ 76

*Power Sharing as Conflicts' Management Tool* ................................ 82

*The Shortcomings of Power Sharing* ................................................ 84

*An Anti-democratic Short-cut* ......................................................... 85

*After Sharing the Cake, What about the Cherry?* ........................... 87

*A Suspicious Coalition, Exclusive Political Outcome* ...................... 87

**CHAPTER 3** ........................................................................................ 90

**Democratic Rotation in High Office** ................................................ 90

Examples of Rotating Presidency and Rotation
of the Outer-space ............................................................. ...................93

*The UN and EU* ................................................................................ 93

*The African Union and the Union of the Comoros* .......................... 95

*Rotating Movement of the Cosmos* ................................................. 96

Conceptual Bases of the Democratic Rotation in High Office.......... ...97

*Strategic Group* ............................................................................... 99

*Conflicting Groups* .......................................................................... 99

*Electoral System with Rotating Candidacy* ................................... 100

*Operating Mode* .............................................................................. 101

Legal and Sociopolitical Safeguards....... ......................................103

*At the National level* ....................................................................... 103

*At the International Level* ............................................................... 103

*Socio-political Safeguards* .............................................................. 105

**CHAPTER 4** ...................................................................................... 108

**Projecting Democratic Rotation into practical cases**........................ 108

Deteriotarized Identities (Rwanda, Burundi, USA, SA) ........ .........108

Geographically Identifiable Identities........ .............................110

Ivory Coast........ ...........................................111

*Strategic and Conflicting Groups* ................................................. 111

*Rotating Cycle in Ivory Coast* ...................................................... 118

Cameroon........ .................................119

*Ethnographic Landscape* ................................................... 119

*Strategic and Conflicting Groups* ..................................... 122

*Electoral Regions in Cameroon* ........................................ 152

*Rotation Cycle in Cameroon* .............................................. 154

**CONCLUSION** ....................................................................... 160

**BIBLIOGRAPHY** .................................................................. 162

**APPENDIXES** ........................................................................ 173

# DEDICATION

*To*
*my wife, Mrs. Tagou Gladisse*
*&*
*our son, Tagou Fowa Mandela*

# ACKNOWLEDGEMENTS

I would, first of all, like to thank a few German institutions, which, each, at a given moment during my university training and professional life has provided an irreplaceable support in Africa and Germany. These include the DAAD, the Heinrich-Boell-Stiftung, the Wilhem-Hahn-und Erben-Stiftung and the EED/Brot für die Welt. In the same vein, I would like to express my gratitude to my professors: David Simo, Lothar Brock, Rainer Tetzlaff and above all, Johan Galtung, who introduced me to the academia of Peace and Development Studies and who, from his position as a leading scholar has put Democratic Rotation into the philosophical footprints of positive transcendence and transformation of meso and mega conflicts in divided societies. I am also very grateful to Prof. Johan Galtung for accepting to write the foreword to the English version of this book. May reverend Professors Emmanuel Anyambod Anya and Timothée Bouba Mbima, former and current Rectors of the Protestant University of Central Africa (PUCA) also find in this book the sign of gratitude for their support since the day I settled on the mythical hill of Djoungolo in 2007 as an assistant lecturer, freshly graduated from the Federal Republic of Germany.

I equally take this opportunity to express my deepest gratitude to Cameroonian forward thinkers, who from the onset, believed in the importance and the need for an academic course in *Peace and Development Studies* pioneered by the FSSIR of PUCA in Africa in three cycles (Bachelor, Master and PhD). These moving spirits have continued to bring invaluable contribution to the training and leadership of Cameroonians and Africans majoring in this course. These professors include inter alia: Daniel Abwa, Jean-Emmanuel Pondi, Tuna Mama, Luc Sindjoun, Nga Dongo Valentin, David Simo, Vincent Ntuda Ebode, Roger Mondoué, Fabien Kange Ewane of blessed memory, etc...

In the past few years, I have had several informal discussions with non-academics that have deeply shaped my thinking as far as this book is concerned. As a result, I am indebted to friends of AEB and CADB associations in Douala; to Caves Encco and UnM (lM); Deux-zéro estudiantine of Omnisport Yaoundé, and all friends of exchange and debate fora Pireco and Alymbo.

May my children, Maguezi Tagou Senphy, Tagou Sana Djuine, Galtung Tagou Nephane and Tagou Fowa Mandela also find in this publication the solace of my absence during the write-up.This also applies to my adopted daughters Samantha and Sandrine Fopa, Carole Matchinda, and my daughter in-law Mrs. Tchinda Linda Christelle.

The financial support of the Network of Protestant Universities of Africa (NPUA) played a decisive role in this publication. Many thanks to my collaborators of the NPUA Executive Secretariat: Mrs. Mireille Belinga, Mr. Edtith Christian Ngoube Ngoube, Mrs. Stéphanie Yakam, Miss. Paule Odette Nani, Miss Anemone Loko Bille Miss Charlotte Konai and Mr. Nathan Awono. As the Executive Secretary, I appreciate their team spirit.

The first French version of this book was published locally in 2017 both by the Protestant University Press and Les Editions du Schabel. Due to its success in the French speaking academic milieu, it became necessary to publish an English version. This idea was proposed and implemented by **Prof. David Tiomajou,** to whom I pay particularly deep tribute. This English version has been proofread by Prof. Divine Che Neba and Cage Banseka. May they accept my sincere gratitude.

Some French and German quotations have been translated into English by the translator **Prof.David Tiomajou**. They are italicized, but not put in inverted commas. Book references are kept in their original language. I do apologize for any inconvenience that this might pose to those who do not feel at home in German and French. The three languages (French, English and German) are the backbone of my academic and scientific adventure. To Almighty be the Glory!


Yaoundé, August 2018                                    Célestin   Tagou

# FOREWORD

"Democratic Rotation in the Head of State Position in Africa" is the title of this important book. It could just as well have ended with "in Europe", focused on the past, and much less like this book focused on the present and the future. The job has been done.

What were they up against in Europe, and now in Africa?

The monarch, of course, the chief of course; deeply entrenched as unquestionable heads; in the state system as the heads of state. Transition to "democratic rotation" – of prime ministers, presidents – took time, and blood, sweat and tears, to put it mildly.

In Europe it was also a step into the unexplored and uncertain; Africa has at least Europe to look at, Europe had nothing.

When we talk about "good kings, bad kings" and "good chiefs, bad chiefs" there are three messages: there are criteria for good and bad, there are kings and chiefs of both kinds, and there is change from one kind to the other but not necessarily every second time. There could be series of one kind only, hoping for long, good series to prevail.

Enters democracy, letting people decide whom they want, directly, – or indirectly via parties and parliaments for instance – as heads. Have a look at the table of contents of this book and see how deeply Tagou takes us into democratic theory and social theory in general.

Africans, like most European countries, are divided ethnically. From a mono-arch or mono-chief to democratic election with a divided electorate deciding is a far step. How did Europe manage?

By pretending that ethnicity has been overridden by citizenship: the new nation-state ethnicity; or by federalism; or by the Swiss formula: a cabinet of 7 divided 3-2-1-1 between German-French-Italian-Ladino speaking, and 2-3-2 by left-middle-right wing. Worth noting!

By reading this book, you are in for an important theoretical and pragmatic solution oriented sociopolitical journey with Tagou as your guide.


**Alfaz Del Pi, July 2018**                    **JOHAN GALTUNG**

# INTRODUCTION

In his academic discourse about good governance, Guy Mhone defines it as the need for the government to fulfill its duty in efficiently and effectively managing governmental institutions, human resources and the financial apparatus in order to meet the objectives of a centered-state or the objectives of a centered-society, or both.[1] And what may hamper or impede this good governance in African countries is, according to Mhone, not only an attitude problem but also the way responsibility, consultation and participation mechanisms are institutionalized within the relationship between those in power and the people. At this level, the main challenge is about the extent to which organizational and institutional structures are there to facilitate good and democratic governance in terms of relationship between the society and the State.[2] Mhone thinks that in order to overcome this challenge the public sector in African states must be re-invented. The necessary condition for re-inventing the public sector in Africa with the aim of implementing good governance in the management of public affairs would be a realistic improvement of political life on this continent where several countries since the 1990s, still fall prey to not only recurrent disputes over different electoral consultations, but even more torn apart by vicious conflicts and ethnic violence whose main stake is the access to the supreme power in order to have the political, economic, natural and other resources under control.

Good governance alone could not in a long term contribute to sustainable development in Africa; that is to positive[3] and perpetual[4]

---

[1] Mhone, Guy C.Z.: Les défis de la gouvernance, de la réforme du secteur public et de l'administration publique en Afrique, University of Witwatersrand Février, 2003. P.11

[2] Ibid., p.6

[3] The concept of peace has a double connotation in the international cooperation world for development and conflict management: Johan Galtung talks of Negative Peace and Positive Peace. Negative Peace refers to the absence of physical and armed conflict. Here, peace is equal to a state of no war. Conversely, the concept of Positive Peace presupposes a multidimensional implementation of social justice, equality, political and individual

peace, if participatory mechanisms in democratic elections do not become institutional, social and political normality that warrants peaceful political rotation. In other words, democratic participation and rotation of power with a real separation of the three powers remain the best political means to ensure good governance and efficient functioning of the public sector in most African countries, where ethnic crush feeds the monopolization of power and at the same time nurtures political patronage and large scale corruption. As Barack Obama once put it, "Africa does not need strong men. It needs strong institutions."[5] And the rotation principle could contribute to the consolidation of the political institutions on the continent. To Professor Mhone's questions: Where is Africa heading to? What are its projects… and what are the necessary means to get us there?[6] It is hard not to believe that Africa has not been able to equip itself with positive peace which is sine qua non for sustainable development. But how do we go about this? This would undoubtedly be through democracy, provided that the contemporary generation of researchers invent or re-invent a model of democracy specific to Africa, one which is fine-tuned with African history, culture, customs and ancestral knowledge. The import, the implementation or better still the copy and paste or the einz zu eins of the Jacobin type of constitutional democracy has been a political and societal mistake in young African States, where the notion of state is not rooted in the existence of a nation with a national consciousness, fully developed and where different democratization processes are very recent. This mistake must be acknowledged and corrected. As once stated by Pondi on RFI "Fifty years after independence, Africans must break up from the copy and paste model and draw from Africa's millenni-

---

freedom of human potentials in line with social and ecological entirety. In a nutshell, Positive Peace is the complete absence of structural and individual violence in a given society and between states at the international level.

[4] The concept "Perpetual Peace" comes from Father Charles Irénée Castel de Saint Pierre, Reference: « Extrait du projet de la paix perpétuelle de l'Abbé de Saint Pierre». In 1795, Kant will talk of « Zum ewigen Frieden »

[5] In his speech addressed to the Ghana's parliament during his first state visit to sub-Saharan Africa,July 11, 2009

[6] Mhone, Guy C.Z. in: op.cit. p.10

um ancestral knowledge in order to take over the past, the present and the future of the continent".[7] Contrary to what Alain Didier Olinga thinks, it is certainly not about re-inventing something different from western type of institutional democracy. We agree that the choice has already been made to the benefit of institutional democracy of liberal constitutionalism. But it is important to move beyond the universal values and principles… of such a political option, where each western institutional democracy, according to its context, has developed a model of socio-political control[8] to articulate and implement these universal values and principles within a given particular realpolitik. This is what has to be captured from this model of democracy which is neither a political regime nor a political system. Here the political system refers to the form of governance which may be despotic, monarchic, dictatorial or democratic etc.…According to Winston Churchill "Democracy is the worst form of government, except for all others".[9]And there are certainly basic principles and values that distinguish the democratic system from other political systems but there is no universal model. This is why each old western democracy, indeed, has developed a model of democracy that allows it to better manage and control the issue of access or withdrawal of the people-drawn legitimacy in the political option of constitutional democracy.

Joseph Owona has proposed that we model the political systems of the geographic space of postcolonial Cameroon to invent the future solution to our institutions. According to him, a chiefdom with alternating dynasties such as Bali-Kumbat in the North-West region of Cameroun could be a model of regional alternation… that consists in a supreme power rotation between the regions of the country: the North, the South, the Far North, the West and the East, thus breaking out from the well-known back and forth game between the North and

---


[7]   Pondi Jean Emmanuel: On RFI in a program with Alain Foka on February 27th,2011.

[8]   Olinga, Alain Didier: « L'Afrique en quête d'une technique d'enracinement de la démocratie constitutionnelle », in: Kamto, Maurice (sd.) L'Afrique dans un monde en mutation. Dynamiques internes, marginalisation internationale ? Paris, Afrédit, 2010 ; P.170,171,176,178

[9]   Winston Churchill: in a "House of common Speech of November 11th, 1947."

the South.[10] But it must be pointed out that questions of the Res publica within the modern State and those of the democratic legitimacy of such an alternation in political power as well as partisan stakes are not accounted for in the approaches to our old sociopolitical organizations, because constitutional democracy is not African. Owona does not tell us how the choice of the owner of the supreme power will be made in the case of Cameroon with political parties while maintaining the parliamentarian aspect in the legitimacy. In such a process one would simply put aside the Republic and democracy, which is almost impossible nowadays.

With regard to democracy and popular legitimacy, the 2010–2017 period has particularly been an all risk period for Africa. More than thirty elections (presidential, parliamentarian, referendum) have taken place within the continent. With these elections, it was expected that the voice of the majority of different people called to vote would be respected and that losers would accept the verdict of the ballotbox. Results obtained here and there show that beyond the great democratic lesson from Senegal, Benin, and Ghana…; the positive outcome from the Gambia and Rwanda, the Ivorian, Gabonese, Congolese and Kenyan political landscape portrayed something else and is still a major challenge to all African intellectuals and Africanists. This challenge is about re-inventing an approach to ethnic-political conflicts management and a democratic model on the African continent. Beyond actors' games and interests in the various post electoral conflicts, there is a real unfinished substantive debate that must be resolved. This debate is about the type or model of democracy that Africa needs with the understanding that there is no universal model of democracy. Due to the political context in which young African states emerged in the 1960s and taking into account the ethnic structure of their different people, this question must be urgently addressed. More than twenty-five years after the collapse of the Berlin wall, the general consensus is that the Jacobin democratic model has its limitations in Africa. This form of government certainly has prin-

---

[10]  Owona, Joseph: Les Systèmes politiques pré coloniaux, Paris, L'Harmattan, 2015, p.95–96

ciples that can become universal (respect of different liberties, universal suffrage, and separation of powers…), but given the historical and universal trajectories of various democracies, in the history of its formulation and even more so of its implementation, since its start in the ancient Greece and more recently in the 1789 French Revolution, it has several models that take into account the historical and cultural circumstances and context in which it is introduced as a regulatory method of political game in a given state. It has been almost unanimously thought that liberal democracy, and even more importantly with its principle of individual freedom of candidacy to people sovereignty, is a guarantee of good governance and accountable leadership at the helm of states. Through the democratic ballot-box, the people would henceforth have the possibility to hold leaders to account when they care less about meeting their basic needs as echoed by Robert McNamara[11], Thomas Sankara[12], Galtung[13] To this, Amartya Sen has added the concept of liberty.[14]

The second finding is that the first fifteen years of the 21st century went down memory lane of the African continent not only as another wasted opportunity for development with regard to the mixed-feeling results of the MDGs[15], but also as a crucial period of military political history of the continent with new patterns of war commonly known as asymmetric and cyber warfare, with side effects which

---

[11]  In the 1973 World Bank conference in Nairobi, McNamara established Health, Nutrition and Education as Human being's basic needs, which must be met to ensure the survival and the dignity of a human being.

[12]  Pondi, Jean-Emmanuel: Thomas Sankara et l'Emergence de l'Afrique au 21°siècle, AfricEveil, Yaoundé 2015. Here, the author shows with specific details that the 8 MDGs were designed and implemented by the pan-Africanist, Thomas Sankara between 1983 and 1987 in the land of People of Integrity, long before they were adopted in September 2000 by the United Nations.

[13]  Galtung, Johan: Transcendance et Transformation des Conflits: une introduction au métier de médiateur, PUPA, 2010, Yaoundé. p.61–88

[14]  Sen, Amartya: Development as Freedom, Oxford University Press, 1999

[15]  MDGs: The 8 Millennium Development Goals were adopted by the UN on September 8th, 2000 at the 55th General Assembly. They constitute a road map that the international community uses in order to resolve issues of poverty, misery, under-development in a well-specified timing. On September 25th, 2015, the MDGs were substituted by 17 Sustainable Development Goals (SDGs) in the UN 70th General Assembly in 2015.

include, among others, non-African military interventions on the continent. As a matter of fact, since the year 2000, Africa has been the hot bed to several events whose impact and scope on the future of the continent in the coming years and centuries are still to be grasped and understood. From disputed elections (Kenya, Zimbabwe, Ivory Coast, DRC, Gabon, Guinea Conakry, Gambia....) to the resurgence of armed force and street driven regimes and military coups at the same time, including the independence of Southern Sudan, armed rebellions and powerful uprising of Wahhabi[16] type of Islamic radicalism (Guinea Conakry, Libya, Mali, CAR, Egypt, Tunisia, Burkina Faso, Nigeria, Cameroon, Chad, Niger...), we are witnessing the invalidity of the international law principles once the sacrosanct of non-interference in the States' internal affairs and their inviolable borders enshrined in the Charter of the former OAU in 1963. In so doing, the African continent has become the ideal testing ground of two concepts adopted by the international community: the United Nation Responsibility to Protect (R2P) and Power Sharing in time of violence. With the blank check that the international community provided France a reason for its recent military interventions in the continent (Ivory Coast with Licorne Operation, Libya with the French-British intervention, Mali with Serval Operation and the CAR with Sangaris Operation, the Sahel G5...)[17], some observers stated that Franceafrique that some people believed dead has never been healthier and boosting that through the past thirty years or so: Hollande

---

[16] Betche, Zachée: Le Phénomène Boko Haram au-délà du radicalisme. L'Harmattan 2016 pp.21–30. Betche presents the three variants of the Muslim Salafism and demonstrates how the third trend born from Mohammed Ibn Abdel Wahhab (1720–1792) serves as a religious inspiration basis to Boko Haram, the Muslim sect.

[17] Besides, these recent interventions, it should be recalled that from 1960 to 2016, the well-known military cooperation agreement signed between France and its former African colonies allowed the French army to intervene more than fifty times on the African continent with varying objectives from assistance to French citizens to loyal regime protection/re-establishment including the overthrow of non-submissive regimes to the metropolis. The Sahel G5 is the sub-regional institutional and strategic coordination framework between 5 countries aiming at fighting against terrorism. It was set up in Nouakchott on February 16th, 2014 and members are: Mali, Mauritania, Burkina Faso, Niger and Chad.

does better than Sarkozy in the words of Shanda Tomne,[18] a Cameroonian political scientist. Whether this hypothesis, spread in public opinion by Afrique Media and various social networks, is confirmed by analysis or not, it is obvious that French interventions disguised in humanitarian interference have been possible and sometimes necessary because of the legendary inability of our states to resolve a sociopolitical equation with three unknown factors: 1 – maintain the integration, the cohesion and national unity; 2 – enable the participation and democratic alternation and 3 – meet citizens' basic needs through a fair redistribution of political and economic resources among ethno-regional or religious groups, which constitute the identity basis of various people whose access or withdrawal to power legitimacy and sovereignty has become an empty shell.

The third mistake which follows the first two is the choice made for **Power Sharing** since the beginning of 1994, between those who want to take power even by arms and those who are looking for ways of monopolizing it and remaining in control even at the expense of identity manipulation and organized killings of uncontrollable populations. From the Arusha agreement in 1993 on the Rwandan crisis to the political agreement of Ouagadougou in 2007 on the Ivorian crisis, including the Sun City agreement on DRC in 2002, those on Zimbabwe and Kenya in 2008, the **Power Sharing** concept has shown its limitations as a resolution method of ethno-political and partisan conflicts in the democratic game in Africa.

There is, therefore, a need for a new model that would not only anticipate conflict escalation upstream, but also would serve as a political way out of any sustainable crisis, should there be any ethnicity or regionalization election result disputes. It is in this mindset that, since 2006, I have been trying to build a theoretical armory around what I referred to at that time as "Demokratisches Rotationsprinzip". Published in Germany in 2006.Given the post electoral political

---

[18]  Tomne, Shanda: Cameroun/RCA: Après la RCA, «la France a des plans contingents pour le Cameroun ». Professor Shanda TONME's clarifying remarks on January, 24th, 2014, consulted on February, 9th, 2016 at 8.45pm in:
http://wmedia.m.cameroon-info.net/stories/0,56764,@,cameroun-rca-apres-la-rca-laquo-la-france-a-des-plans-contingents-pour-le-camero.html, Consulté le 09/02/2016 à 20h45

stalemates arround the continent and comforted by the positive effects of the minimalist application of rotation within some international organizations, in the Comoros Islands, in the party in power in Nigeria[19] and within some protestant churches in Cameroon and DRC[20], I thought that, with this political essay, it would be useful to relaunch the debate on this problem by giving the intellectual and political milieu the opportunity to appreciate the Democratic rotation model. The model takes into account African societies' sociocultural and historic realities into the democratic game thereby making and the theoretical effort not to confine African conflict management in counterproductive calculations of national cake sharing prescribed by the Power Sharing concept.

Before elaborating on the conceptual and theoretical framework of this model, it is first of all worthwhile, to scientifically give an operational definition of Ethnicity and State concepts, showing the links that they have with the concepts of Clan, Tribe, Community, People and Race. Secondly, I will embark on a critical analysis of the western type of liberal democracy and the concept of Power Sharing, showing the limitations of their import into the African context; and thirdly, I will present the Democratic Rotation model illustrating it with some case studies, including Ivory Coast and Cameroon in details[21].These two countries have been specifically chosen as case

---

[19]  Political power rotation takes place within the Popular Democratic Party (PDP) in Nigeria between the North and the South, between Muslims and Christians. It is an unwritten principle whose merit is to limit ethno-regional conflicts within the party. That is a minimal version of Rotation Democracy because the latter model goes beyond the only party in power and equally calls on opposition political parties thus putting all political parties in a momentum that takes into account socio-cultural, regional and identity constraints that cannot be ignored.

[20]  In the EEC (Eglise Evangélique du Cameroun), the UEBC (Union des Eglises Baptistes du Cameroun)…and the ECC (Eglise du Christ au Congo). What is happening in the EEC today does not put into question the relevance of the Rotation at the head of this church. The conflict would have had a different meaning or become more serious if it had been a Bamoun-Sawa conflict, Bamoun-Bamileke or Sawa-Bamileke. Both are Sawa sons. Even though the Sawa origin of one is slightly challenged, it remains a micro-conflict, thus easily manageable.

[21]  Further studies could extend to other countries of the continent that have the same socio-political difficulties between ethnic groups, national integration and democracy

studies in order to demonstrate how Democratic Rotation would have prevented the Ivorian crisis and how, contrary to the Ouagadougou Political Agreement (OPA) outcomes, it would have been a transcendence and transformation of the conflict between Laurent Gbagbo and Alasane Dramane Ouattara, with a zero sum option resolution for the latter, who won all with nothing left for the former, and how this situation resulted in a negative transcendence. The Cameroon case study is equally interesting, not only because the country has been a haven of peace until the vicious attacks of Boko Haram sect in 2013 and the resurgence of the Anglophone problem in 2016,[22] but because, there is the need to anticipate in Cameroon not only what happened in Ivory Coast and DRC, but also in Kenya, Zimbabwe and in Sudan. Cameroon is a strategic country which so far had been an example of political stability, cohesion, ecumenical and inter-religious dialogue and described by Galtung as"…a message, a very positive message".[23] But since 2003, Cameroon has, ironically, become a sort of "Pressure Cooker"[24] showing permanent signs of meso, macro, mega conflicts' escalating[25] into violence based on identity divides which have become intractable because of the manipulation of naturally acquired or socially constructed identities by a dangerous sociopolitical cronyism in these times of constitutional democracy.

---

[22] Details and our analysis of the Anglophone problem are presented later in the study.

[23] Galtung, Johan: « The intrinsic linkage between Conflict, Development, Civilization and Peace in 21 Century » in Tagou, Célestin (sd.): The dynamics of conflict, Peace and Development in African Societies, from local to international, Yaoundé, PUPA 2010, p.17

[24] Dougueli, Georges « Cameroun sous le Couvercle de la Cocotte-Minute » in Jeune Afrique N°2963–2964 du 22 Octobre au 4 Novembre 2017, p.34,39

[25] For details on the typology of conflicts in Cameroon, refer to: Tagou, Célestin:" Managing ethno-regional diversities in African states: Western peace paradigms versus African peace philosophy and a political way out" in Kayser, Christian&Djateng, Flaubert: Working for Sustainable Peace in Cameroon. CPS/EED, Bafoussam, Berlin 2011, pp.38–47

# CHAPTER 1

## Key Concepts and connotation in the 21st Century

As stated earlier, I will attempt in this section to provide a conceptual clarification of the terms: Ethnic group, Ethnicity and Nation/State in order to make a category-based distinction between these concepts and those referred to as: Tribe/Clan, Community, People and Race and finally, to up-date how they are perceived in the 21st century and scientifically show how they fit within the conceptual framework of Democratic Rotation as political mechanisms for positive transformation of ethno-regional diversities and conflicts within a given state.

### Ethnic Group and Ethnicity

According to Max Weber, the German sociologist, the concept of ethnicity and the derived terminologies should not be part of scientific vocabulary. In his opinion, they are so vague and inaccurate that they cannot qualify for usage in a rigorous scientific approach.[26]Weber's position is understandable in the historical context of the 19th century and the beginning of the 20th century. But at the beginning of the 1990s, it was noted that Weber's warnings had only remained on paper. The vague and inaccurate ethnicity concept and the derived terminologies have comfortably settled not only into politics but in all other fields of social sciences. Nowadays, any social or human science that does not take close interest in this phenomenal concept, which accounts for ethnic cleansing, genocide which have put several states on the brink of implosion and socio-political disintegration from Africa to Europe, from Asia to America, would be an admission of failure. It has, therefore, to be taken care of from all angles. To this end, it is necessary to revisit the different theoretical approaches developed in social sciences in order to better understand this phe-

---

[26] Weber, Max: Wirtschaft und Gesellschaft. Tübingen 1922 p. 224

nomenon. It is, therefore, equally necessary to rebuild the various political and scientific speeches on ethnic group and ethnicity; the way these terms came into the world of science in order to bring out all the various definitional approaches that have been made available and to see what distinguishes them from the related categories such as the Clan, Tribe, Community, People, Race, Nation and State. At the end of this chapter the question related to the connotation of these concepts in the 21[st]century will be addressed. Do they still refer to the same sociopolitical realities as in the 18th and 19th century of European history?

**The Advent of the Terms in Social Sciences and Politics**

A look at the history of the scientific literature on the terms ethnic group/ethnicity shows that the strides made by the concept to find its way into politics and social sciences are intimately close to the history of the relationship between Europeans and other people. Colonial conquests went together with the awakening of a special interest in European research to better know and understand the people of color, their cultures and customs. That is how a new scientific field of study called **Ethnology** was developed within western universities. The focus of research in this new field, whose pseudo-scientific nature has widely been demonstrated by Theophile Obenga[27], was the study of non-western people, their traditions, their social organizations, their habits and customs, their way of life with the nature, how they eat, how they make love etc. This is what was referred to in England as *Social Anthropology*, known in the USA under the concept of *Cultural Anthropology* and in the German-speaking world as *"Völkerkunde"*. If mankind was the general focus of anthropology, and mainly the human in western societies, as a sub-branch of anthropology, ethnology purports to be a science that would allow settlers to systematically assess the culture and the social structures of dominated and colonized primitive people. Until the end of the 19th century, *ethnology* meant *the study of the races* in English. In 1895, the Encyclopedia of Ethnology still divided the world population in

---

[27] Obenga, Théophile: Cheikh Anta Diop, Volney et le Sphnix. Présence Africaine, 1996. Pp.27–45

four primary groups which were: Homos Ethiopicus, Mongolicus, Americanus and Cacasius. Chapman could thus see in the connotations of the word ethnicity all the *"Terms relate to the discourse built around the idea of race, for which ethnos has been no more than a redundant synonym. Ethnology was the Study of races."*[28]

It is towards the middle of the 20th century that groups of people could be considered ethnic groups regardless of the color of the skin, that is, their race. On the African continent, in cooperation with colonial masters, European anthropologists and ethnologists classified colonized people into inviolable ethnic groups, giving them identities and creating names wherever there wasn't any.[29] This was done with the sole purpose of controlling them better, dominating and making them liable. This strategy was unfortunately transferred into African modern States. It has to be pointed out that at the beginning of the colonial expansion; colonized people were first called *people* or *Nations*. It is with the establishment of real intentions of the colonial politics with its exploitation and domination structures that the word *Tribe* was used in politics and became part of the anthropologists' and ethnologists' vocabulary. In the 1940s, the concept *tribe* in the anthropology milieu was gradually shifted into the concept of *ethnic group*. Such a classification of social aggregates into ethnic groups has been one aspect of the literature on ethnicity while scientific research on groups' behavior with regard to their common identity has been the other.

Following the Anthropology field, it was the turn of Sociology to integrate the concepts of *ethnic group and Ethnicity* in its vocabulary. The concept is used in Anthropology to refer to foreign groups (non-European) out of Europe, but in Sociology the concept refers to a foreigner within his/her own group. In *"Wirtschaft und Gesellschaft" Max* Weber makes an exception using the word in a

---

[28] Chapman, Malcon/McDonald, Maryon/Toukin, Elisabeth: Introduction. History and Social Anthropology in: Tonkin/McDonald/Chapmann (Hg.) 1989 p.14

[29] The origin of the word Bamileke for example is a pure invention of the German colonizer. It does not exist in any dialects spoken by the people known today in Cameroon as Bamileke.

more universal connotation despite his own reservations regarding its inclusion into scientific vocabulary. From this moment, Poutignat and Streiff-Fenart point out that the descriptions of the terms *tribe* and *tribalism* are no longer approved unanimously in western anthropological circles: *the terms tribe and tribalism are severely criticized for the stereotyped and pejoratives visions of Africans that they carry along and several anthropologists are suggesting their rejection for the benefit of the terms ethnic group and ethnicity indiscriminately applicable to all societies. With this in mind, the concept of ethnicity expresses the unity of a universal and omnipresent social phenomenon.*[30]

It should be pointed out here that it was first in Anglo-Saxon societies that the use of the term *ethnic group* settled in sociology, and notably in American sociology circles. Until then, it has not totally lost its character of undermining minority groups by the dominant and/or majority group that refer to less influent and minority groups by sub-categories. Here, one would have thought that the existence of ethnic groups was a temporary phenomenon as they would have been assimilated in the modernization process of societies. At the level of research in the field for the case studies, there was a slight paradigm shift in the knowledge objectives, mostly with regard to English anthropologists who work on Africa.

Beyond traditional anthropology, the interaction between ethnic groups with respect to social changes, migrations and urbanization are becoming a research area.[31] In the 1960s, the interest in ethnicity was due to its political challenge and impact on newly independent young states. At the same time, the American Sociology had begun to consider ethnic groups as constitutive components of a modern society. Research works are not only restricted to the internal behavior of ethnic groups, but much more on social interaction of ethnic groups among themselves and between groups and the State. This is how the political interest in ethnicity became predominant in re-

---

[30] Poutignat, Philippe & al.: Théories de l'éthnicité. Presse Universitaires de France, 1995 p.32

[31] Lentz, Carola in: op. cit.(1994), pp.120–121

search. This prompted Thompson to make the following remarks: *"New journals devoted to the ethnicity proliferated, universities established ethnic studies programs by the score."[32]* In 1975 Glazer and Moynihan published the famous volume on *"Ethnicity, Theory and Experience"* in which they demonstrated that the concept of Ethnicity[33] had appeared in scientific publications in the 1950s. The same volume also contained ethnological analyses on Western, Russian and Chinese societies as well as Third World societies which made the concept become a universally observable phenomenon in all human societies and no longer only within defeated, under slavery societies in imperialistic battles. With regard to the control of political power, emphasis is laid on the conflictual nature of the social interaction of ethnic groups among themselves on negative stereotype background and with the State. This is why the phenomenon must be talked only in an interdisciplinary perspective. Thus, restricting it only to Anthropology and Sociology would make us lose sight of the challenges, impact and political implications of issues related to ethnicity. Galser and Moynihan were themselves, political scientists.

In German Anthropology, the concept became important in research in the 1960s. The ethnologist, Wilhelm E. Mühlmann, saw the emergence of ethnic groups within contradictions, stemming from various human races' meetings and mixtures.[34] The *ethnic minority* concept had been used in the German Federal Republic (GFR) as in the United States of America (USA) and England to refer to groups of peoples from migration. Thus, thirty-six groups of people were registered in the emigration services under the term ethnicity.[35] Political xenophobes and far rightists did not waste time in picking up the

---


[32]   Thompson, Richard H.: Theories of Ethnicity. A critical Appraisal, New York: Greenwood Press. 1989.

[33]   Glazer &al.: Ethnicity, Theory and Experience, Cambridge, Mass, Harvard University Press, 1975

[34]   Mühlmann, Wihelm E: Rassen Ethnien, Kulturen. Moderne Ethnologie, Neuwied: Luchterland 1964.pp. 83–97

[35]   Schmalz-Jacobsen, Cornelia / Hansen, Georg: Ethnische Minderheiten in der Bundesrepublik Deutschland. Ein Lexikon, München. Beck 1995.

concept, giving it a political connotation thus making it a major electoral challenge with regard to political integration or exclusion of immigrants into industrialized societies.

In France, it was later in the 1970s and 1980s that the concept settled into academic and political circles. Until then, the concept had not yet had the importance that it enjoyed in the Anglo-Saxon scientific world as stated earlier; Poutignart and Streiff-Fenart clearly stated that *the term ethnicity has a completely new usage in the French scientific literature. Despite its introduction into French academic circles as from 1981…it has practically remained unused in ethnological or sociological vocabulary…the interethnic area has long represented the blind spot of French anthropology.*[36] This is justified by the lack of public interest in this scientific research branch. As a consequence, there have been no public subventions to carry out analyses on the interactions between ethnic groups and the relationship that they have with the state. Given the Jacobin dogmatism and the legendary unity and much more unicity of the Great French Nation, any scientific piece of writing on the diversity of the French population would have resulted in no opportunity to gain an academic and political audience. Literature on ethnic groups and ethnicity was therefore ignored and stifled in all areas. Political and scientific consequences of this throttling of research on the phenomenon of *ethnic group and ethnicity* in France had severe repercussions in former French colonies where ethnic groups were literally sacrificed on the altar of the emerging new nations in progress and which later became a challenge to power with the advent of democracy. For example, and like many of his counterparts, the first president of Cameroon, father *of the nation* clearly stated, in 1964, this political option, influenced by the metropolis, when he wrote *National unity means that on the nation building site, there are neither Ewondo, nor Douala, Bamilike, Boulou, Foulbe, Bassa etc… but everywhere and always Cameroonians…*[37] Questions about what is a Cameroonian? What

---

[36] Poutignat, Philippe/Jocelyne Streiff-Fenart op.cit. p.21–22.

[37] Ahidjo, Ahmadou: Contribution à la construction nationale. Présence Africaine, Paris, 1964.p.29

does it mean to be a Cameroonian? How do Cameroonians distinguish themselves from other people, have remained sustainably unanswered. The term Cameroonian needed a bookmarked content for a mythical belief. It is President Paul Biya that suggested one of the answers to the concept of national integration in which the Cameroonian nation does no longer see itself in terms of unicity and standardization but in terms of multi-cultural syncretism.[38] But this integrative approach of Biya has remained in political discourse to date.

It is the end of the cold war that marked a turning point in the interest given to the concept of ethnic group and ethnicity mostly at the political level in under-developed countries, mostly in former French colonies. The academia is not left behind: sociology and social sciences will totally invest in this new research area, which so far has seemed to be the private ground of mostly Anglo-Saxon ethnologists and anthropologists. In political sciences, the concept of *ethnic group* and ethnicity would become even more important as they are at the heart of new analytical perspectives on the causes of conflicts which, formerly, were often labeled as the extension of the ideological conflict between the East and the West known as internationalized civil wars by Bercovith[39] or as meso intra-State conflicts with macro and mega colors by Galtung.[40] With the end of the cold war, the terms *ethnic group/ethnicity* provide new reading keys to conflicts not only in Africa, but everywhere, where ideological division went hand in hand with sphere of influence. This is testified by the number of research institutes and academic papers whose research projects focused on the concept of ethnic group and ethnicity. Thus, *the International Sociological Association* set up a research group called *Research Committee on Ethnic, Race and Migration Relations;* and the *International Political Sciences Association* (IPSA) *put in place* the

---

[38] Biya, Paul: Pour le Libéralisme Communautaire, Éditions Marcel Fabre, Lausanne, 1987.

[39] Bercovitch, Jacob & al: Regional conflict to international conflict, Congressional Quarterly, 2004, pp.1–46

[40] Galtung, Johan: Transcendance et Transformation des Conflits: Une Introduction au métier de médiateur, traduit de l'anglais au français par Tagou, Célestin, PUPA, Yaoundé, 2010.

*Research Committee on Politics and Ethnicity*. In the 1990s, a new program called *Ethnic and Nationalist Conflict Program* was set up in Johan Galtung's *International Peace Research Institute in Oslo* (PRIO) while at the same time, the *London School of Economics and Political Science* was launching the *Association for the Study of Ethnicity and Nationalism*. Even in Moscow, in 1993, the *Ethno-Political Studies Center* focused its research on the theme *Settlement of Ethnic Conflicts in Post-Soviet Society*...[41] All these research centers also create scientific reviews to publish their research findings on ethnic group and ethnicity and equally organize several conferences on the issue. The post-cold war's most important findings of this scientific rush on the ethnic group and ethnicity concept are a few definitional essays of the terms ethnic group and ethnicity, which, according to Max Webber should never have been part of scientific vocabulary as stated earlier.

In an attempt to grasp the scientific meaning of the concept of *ethnic group/ethnicity*, a discussion will arise between two main approaches of definitions namely: the essentialist (even deterministic) and constructivist approaches. Theoretical discussions between the pros and cons of any of the approaches will also throw little light on the connotative differentiation between the concepts and closely related terms such as *race, tribe, community and nation*.

## What is an Ethnic Group?

In ancient Greece, the word *Ethnos* was already used to make a distinction between us and others. It was used to refer to foreign people and warriors or animals with regard to the Greek people who were said to be more civilized and superior to foreigners. In ancient Rome, the term *Ethnos* was equally used to refer to peripheral provinces, thus making a clear difference with the capital that was at the center. Right from its etymological origin, the term *ethnic group* therefore had a very heavy negative connotation. The term *Ethnikos* was used to refer to barbarians and pagans. Therefore, the German Africanist and anthropologist Carola Lentz concluded that the concept *Ethnic*

---

[41] Tagou, Célestin: op.cit. 2006, pp.82–84.

*group* and related terms operate in an *Us/You* dichotomy, and often refer to others in terms of inferior and primitive civilization.[42]This concept will be used in England with the same connotation until the middle of the 19th century.[43]

First of all, it has to be noted that in several studies devoted to this issue, authors followed Max Webber's reservations by refusing to define the term *ethnic group*. And Cohen noticed this towards the end of the 1970s when he said: "*Most people using the term ethnicity find definitions unnecessary. Isajiew looked at 65 studies of ethnicity in sociology and anthropology and found only 13 that defined that term*".[44] Poutignat and Streiff-Fenart made the same conclusion in their study of 1988. They consider that one should not be impressed by the abundance of literature of the 1990s. In several studies, the concept is more described than defined: *the overwhelming literature on ethnicity should not create illusion. In the majority of cases, the term ethnicity is more used as descriptive category making it possible to resolve a problem of another nature...rather than a sociological concept helping to define a scientific object. The definition review suggested by Isajiew in 1974 highlighted the imprecision and the heterogeneity of the content of the notion... most of the reviews had no explicit definition and a few definitions put forward all looked vague and heteroclite.*[45]

The fact remains that, according to Astrid Lenz, the term ethnicity is derived from ethnic group and refers to a sense of ownership.[46] It would, however, be simplistic to merely accept such a definition from Astrid Lenz. As mentioned earlier, the controversy on the defi-

---


[42] Lentz, Carola: "Tribalismus" und Ethnizität in Afrika: eine Forschungsüberblick, das Arabische Buch, Berlin 1994; p.117 Die Konstruktion von Ethnizität, Rüddiger Köppe Verlag; Köln 1998. p.31 et p.627

[43] Eriksen, Thomas Hylland: Ethnicity and Nationalism. Anthropological Perspectives, London: Pluto 1993, p.4

[44] Cohen, Ronald: Ethnicity: problem and Focus in Anthropology, in: Annual review of Anthropology, Vol. 7, 1978, pp. 379–403. p.385.

[45] Poutignat, Philippe: op.cit. p.93.

[46] Lentz, Astrid: Ethnizität und Macht. Ethnische Differenzierung als Struktur und Prozeß sozialer Schließung im Kapitalismus, Köln: Papy Rossa. 1995. p.22.

nition of the *ethnic group/ethnicity* concept can be better grasped through the authors' classification between those who seek to use objective criteria (essentialists…) and those in favour of subjective categories (constructivists…).

## *The Essentialist Approach*

We must reiterate that before Barth,[47] attempts to answer the question "What is an ethnic group" were fundamentally based on an essentialist approach.[48] The so-called objective approach represented by a small number of authors is the starting point of the theoretical discussion on *ethnic group/ethnicity*. As early adopted in Anglo-Saxon social sciences, the terms ethnic group and ethnicity was equally introduced, but lately in the scientific literature of the French language.[49] The premises for this approach are, thus, found in Kallen's[50] work which already demonstrated that hereditary resemblance and the sense of ownership to a group were the basis of group definition and differentiation. Members of a group have the same ancestors from whom they inherited a culture that connects them. The word *essential* was first introduced into the literature in 1957 by Shils. He used it to identify and to show the importance of the primary group in the integration processes of social reproduction.[51] According to Shils' observations, in everyday life the simple man is not

---

[47] Barth, Fredrik: Ethnic Groups and Boundaries: The social organization of culture Difference; Oslo/Bergen/Tromso, 1969

[48] Several authors think that this approach is out of date. However, it has to be presented here as, it is, as a matter of fact, the starting point which gives way to subsequent development and it is this fixed perception of ethnicity that raises problems in diverse societies in the middle of democratization process.

[49] Carola Lentz(1994) ; Philippe Poutignat et Jocelyne Steiff-Fenart (1998).

[50] It is generally believed that Shils (1957) is the father of the essentialist theory, but the very first basic development of this conception are found in Kallen's essays on cultural diversity published in 1915 under the title: Democracy and the Melting-Pot in: The nation, February 18, 1915, contained in: H.M. Kallen (ed.): Culture and Democracy in the United States, New York, Boni et Liveright, 1924. Nevertheless, the term comes from Shils who used it in 1957 to strengthen his thesis on the need for basic groups to integrate and regenerate the global society. "Essential links" have an indescribable meaning like the one assigned to kingship.

[51] Shils E.op.cit.

guided by ideologies but by a set of primary values that he shares with his group's members. This essential sense of ownership serves as the foundation of the natural relationship that connects the individual to the group. Like in a family relationship, the cultural and essential link is of paramount importance to the group members and serves as the foundation to their sense of ownership and solidarity.

Following Shils' theses, the American sociologist, Brewton Berry suggested the following definition for the term *ethnic group*: *"The ethnic group is a human group, bound together by ties of cultural homogeneity"*.[52] According to him, the existence of an ethnic group implies the existence of cultural particularities commonly shared by all the group members. The sharing of a common language, common religious belief and common origin is added to the cultural homogeneity. Such items of primary ownership and belief would be re-used in several ethnological studies to show the fundamental aspects of the ethnic identity. Ethnic identity is, therefore, primary; the individual is born with it and shares it with other group members. It is made up of some physical characteristics, names, religious affiliation and all the cultural elements passed down from generation to generation. According to this approach, we have to admit that ethnic identity is embedded in an emotional feeling of ownership to a kinship community linked by what Durkheim calls *mechanical solidarity.*[53] Members, thus, share the same biological origin that provides the paramount sense of belonging with an inexplicable and mesmerizing mythical character. Here, the ethnic identity is at the same time essentialist as the identification to the group becomes a virtual forum in which group members, even without seeing one another, without knowing each other, interact and share the same emotions and demand a common history. It is a safe place where the individual does not feel alone, where he/she can escape from loneliness and wherever he/she can seek refuge when threatened. As brothers and sisters, members of the same group mutually support each other and protect

---

[52]  Berry, Brewton: Race Relations: The Interaction of Ethnic and Racial Groups, Boston: Houghton Mifflin. 1951. p.75

[53]  Durkheim, Emile in: Preston, P.W: Development Theory, an Introduction, Blackwell Publishing 1996, p.82–98

themselves against outside groups (out-groups). It is a community of blood the individual belongs to, from birth whether he/she likes it or not. The sociologist, Yinger concludes that the existence of an ethnic group abides by the following criteria which are objectively identifiable: *"language, religion, race and ancestral homeland with its related culture; the members also perceive themselves that way; and they participate in shared activities built around their (real or mythical) common origin or culture."*[54]Language, religion, race and the ancestral soil are the constitutive features of an ethnic group that are objectively observable. In a nutshell, the foundation of an ethnic group presupposes the existence of either a community in language or of origin or culture, in short, a culture within which emotional links between members are created and maintained. There would be no cultural variations and, thus, only human aggregates that essentially share a common culture. The concept of ethnic group, here, is assigned a static dimension and an immutable natural feature. Ethnicity, as such, becomes the essential and deterministic basic element of group identity. The ethnic group, in turn, becomes the best haven where the individual feels safe as it is the place that would never reject him and where he/she would never feel lonely.[55] Here, it is believed that *Ethnicity label = a way of life = a real group.*[56]

The socio-biological version of this theoretical approach of ethnicity also known as objective version comes from Pierre Van den Berghe. According to its biological reductionism, human societies are linked by their members' own interests taken individually. Ethnic feelings and behaviors that determine them result from the genetically programed tendency to do relatives favor at the expense of *outsiders*.[57]In other words, each individual would biologically inherit from the identity group in which he/she is born, he/she cannot do anything

---

54  Yinger, J. Milton: Intersecting strands in the theorisation of race and the ethnic relations, in Rex, John and Mason, David (Hg.): Theories of Race and Ethnic Relations, Cambridge University Press, 1986 p.20–41. p.22.

55  Herold R. Isaacs (1975) in Carola Lentz op.cit. P. 119

56  Poutignat, Philippe/Steiff-Fenat, Jocelyne op. cit. p.68

57  Van den Berghe P.L., Race and ethnicity: a sociobiological perspective in Ethnic and Racial Studies, 1,4, 1978, p.401–411.

about it and would be more likely to have an in-born preference for the members of his/her ethnic group (ethnocentrism) while excluding others that must be destroyed as dangerous ones (ethno-fascism).

## *The Constructivist Approach*

As mentioned earlier, the essentialist school of thought is the starting point of the theoretical discussion on *ethnic group and ethnicity*. Approaches that come after are therefore criticism levelled against essentialists. Thus, following, Barth,[58] a number of approaches will flourish all aiming at defining ethnic groups as instrumental groups subjectively constructed and maintained for their pragmatic utility or as means used to gain collective or individual advantages.[59]From all prospects, this criticism can be summarized in one thing: the constructivist approach that falls back to individual and non-collective criteria of definition. It blames essentialists to be unable to explain the feature of the essentialist links that connect the group members. According to this school of thought, the origin of an ethnic group can be traced back to the subjective belief that an individual has about belonging to a group. The individual, therefore, has a belonging choice. He/she is not connected to the group by a mythical filiation or in blood. Here, ethnicity refers to a community built on the background of a political action in which rational socialization is expressed through the feeling of individual belonging. An ethnic group is, thus, seen as a social phenomenon that builds itself in various contexts of social, economic and political interaction. It is in this respect that Frederick Barth reinforces Weber's[60] theses by bringing out the fact that ethnic group members use: *"ethnic identities to categorize themselves and others for purposes of interactions, they form ethnic groups in this organizational sense"*.[61] According to Barth, ethnicity is only the result of a social fact of barriers' construction stemming from the self-description of oneself and the perception that one has

---

[58]   Barth, Fredrik: Ethnic Groups and Boundaries: The social organization of culture Difference; Oslo/Bergen/Tromso, 1969.

[59]   Barth, Fredrik: op.cit.

[60]   Weber, Max: op.cit., p.129

[61]   Barth, Fredrik: op.cit.

about the other. In this respect, ethnic groups may be built from the categorization made by dominant groups. The concept has become a big political challenge in pluralistic societies. Here, the constructivist or instrumentalist feature of ethnicity clearly operates as a mobilizing factor in the political fight for the control of power and resources in a given State.

The elite plays an important role in the process of ethnic factor political instrumentalization, since it manipulates the mythical feeling of belonging to mobilize the alleged members of its group to support them in the political arena and, if necessary, to destroy their political opponents. Berman underlines the fact that more often, the elite use the work of sociologists and anthropologists to try to provide a scientific basis to their political speech. Berman writes: "*At one level, the political salience and instrumental character of ethnicity is manifested in its deliberate activation as a combination of identity, interest and common action ... Before ethnicity is the basis for political mobilisation and action, it must be a work of intellectual construction, an imagining or invention of a common history, language and culture, typically expressed in oral or written texts combining and reworking both old and new elements*".[62] Glazer and Moynihan are of the opinion that objective criteria of an ethnic group definition such as religion, language of common origin can be interpreted in many different ways and that the only reference point remains in political objectives. The so-called group solidarity is rightly used to mobilize members in the implementation of political objectives essentially beneficial to the elite.[63]

Supplementary studies on the instrumentalization of ethnicity have been further developed by Africanists to contradict the essential explanation of the phenomenon of tribalism in Africa. In post-colonial African States, ethnicity was perceived as the identification basis of groups of populations in political competition. The tribal or tribalism phenomenon, thus, becomes, according to Berman, the political ex-

---


[62]  Berman, Bruce: Ethnicity, Patronage and the african state: The politics of uncivil nationalism in: African Affairs vol. 97, Nr. 388, July 1998. p.312.

[63]  Glazer&al.: op.cit

pression of the ethnicity concept: *"In African political language 'tribalismus' stigmatizes all social and political manifestation of ethnicity".*[64] To defend their political and economic interests, populations fall back on their ethnic origin. In this regard, an ethnic group becomes a societal construction, politically maintained and manipulated. It becomes a political weapon for the elite. It should, however, be noted that such a political construction and manipulation of the ethnicity are not only a reality of the post-colonial State. Following their policy of divide and rule, colonial powers built their system of colony exploitation and domination using colonized population's ethnic differences and nursing resulting conflicts. Here, the ethnicity and ethnic groups as well as their reference are the result of a voluntary or unconscious construction.

Another problem that arises is therefore that of the difference between the individual political interests and aspirations and community, that is, between the sociopolitical interest of an individual and those of the group that he/she pretends to defend. According to Agbu Osita's analysis, this difficulty in drawing the line between the individual and the community has had implications on the different democratization processes in African countries.[65] In the different versions of this approach, individual objectives and strategies, collective fights for the accumulation of resources, as well as the monopolization of political power take a particular prominence. There are several versions of this constructivist approach to ethnicity.

*Interest group theories*: Ethnic identities and ideologies are maintained to exercise influence over social and economic policies. Conflict situations between individuals with the same material interests create a sort of group solidarity. Bell rightly considers that the strength of the ethnicity element is that it allows the combination of interests and affective relations. It mobilizes less abstract and more recognizable cultural symbols than the class and appeals to powerful

---

[64] Berman, Bruce: op.cit. p.306

[65] Agbu, Osita A.: Ethnicity and Democratisation in Africa, Challenges for politics and development. Discussion Paper 62. Nordiska Afrikainstitutet, Uppsala, 2011, p.10.

emotions.[66] This approach as noted by Philippe Poutignat and Jocelyne S.F. is therefore not radically against the essentialist theory. It acknowledges the special feature of ethnic links but studies in depth its strategic use in politics in a given society.

*Rational choice theories*: The criticism of essentialist theories is harsher at this level. It is no longer the involuntary membership and the unconscious internalization of group values that constitute the definitional benchmarks for group members, but the fact that ethnic groups come up contrariwise when individuals cannot seek some goods through strategies of individual competitions; and that they consciously or rationally fall back on the ethnic element to claim resources.[67]

*Neo-Marxist theories*: here it is thought that the capitalist tendency to exploit labor by setting its price as low as possible does create division between workers depending on their ethnic or racial origin and not on biases against people of color or members of a given ethnic group. This approach shows that the antagonism between the immigrants and nationals in industrialized societies (even between natives and non-natives in large cities, industrial and agricultural development poles in Africa)[68] finds a basis in the segmentation of the labor market. Sharing with the instrumentalists the conception that ethnic groups are defined by material, political and economic interests, Marxist theories rather consider that ethnicity is a form of social adherence in competition with the ruling class. The class consciousness being stronger than that of ethnicity, the ruling class (the elite) uses ethnicity to divide and mobilize populations into open conflict ac-

---

[66] Bell D., Ethnicity and social Change in N. Glazer et D.P. Moyniham(eds), Ethnicity, Theory and Experience, Cambrige, Mass, Harvard University Press, 1975, p.141–174. et Gordon M: Human nature, class and ethnicity, New York, Oxford University Press, 1978.

[67] Possibilities of applying the rational choice theory to ethnic and racial relationships were the most developed by Michael Banton. For criticism levelled on this approach, refer to: Philippe Poutignat and Jocelyne in op.cit P.110–113.

[68] Tagou, Célestin: Les migrations intra-africaines et leurs impacts sur la paix et le développement en Afrique Sub-saharienne in Simo, David (sd): Problématiques migratoires en contexte de globalisation, Les Grandes Editions, Yaoundé 2014 pp.159–184

cording to ethnic identity to defend economic and political interests of the ruling class.[69] The ruling class thus falls back on ethnicity to cause conflicts within the State in the form of class struggle.

*Neo-culturalist approaches*: Philippe Poutignat and Jocelyne S.F. use this term to refer to the approach of different authors that are radically against traditional conceptions of culture as an integrated entity, while focusing, however, on cultural aspects of ethnicity. Authors that disapprove of the essentialist thesis, consider the cultural dimension as the focal point for ethnicity. Here, ethnicity is perceived as a process by which individuals exchange ideas on human diversity, through cultural differences, thus trying at the same time to resolve issues of meaning. Research is no longer focused on *how members of X group perceive members of Y group and behave with them*, but it seeks to know *how people define and identify the X or Y features.*[70]

*Ethnicity as a social interaction form*: Contrary to the essentialists, interactionist theories consider ethnicity as a continuous process of dichotomization or opposition between members and outsiders that must be expressed and accepted in social interaction. According to Barth, the existence of ethnic groups depends on the maintenance of their boundaries. Here, it is about knowing how the different types of dichotomization between members and outsiders are produced and maintained. The categorical awarding and interaction process is at the heart of the analysis. This approach, therefore, postulates the cultural contact and the mobility of people. Ethnicity is no longer perceived as a natural anthropological stability that serves as a social organization foundation for individuals sharing a common language and a common culture, but rather as a social concept referring to a group of individuals that describe themselves according to some subjective criteria that distinguish them from others. Ethnicity becomes a fictitious community, an artificially created construction, thus variable through historical evolution given that boundaries between ethnic groups are tangible.

---

[69] Agbu, Osita A. In: op.cit. pp 16–17.

[70] Drummond L., The Cultural continuum: a Theory of Intersystem, Man, vol 15, n° 2, 1980,.cité d'après Philippe Poutignat in op. cit. p.121.

Without getting into the limitations of these approaches in capturing the complex anthropological reality of ethnicity, we, all the same, notice that either way, the need for identity is an issue. The individual has the tendency to identify him/herself with regard to a group. According to essentialists, this identity is cultural and based on what individuals inherit from their ancestors, while for the constructivists, the identity results from what individuals do here and now and not what they have been in the past.[71]

It must, therefore, be noticed that an intrinsic ambiguity of the terms *ethnic group and ethnicity* is on-going. Debates around the concepts, fueled since the 1970s, have not allowed for a general definition of ethnicity. And Max Weber concludes: *"it is certain that in this process the collective term 'ethnic' would be abandoned, for it is unsuitable for a really rigorous analysis."* [72] But taking into account the fact that this category has progressively penetrated the mind of actors and observers (the politician and the scientist), Carola Lentz- who uses the concept not only as an analytical category meeting all the criteria of scientific rigor, but rather in terms of a multifaceted concept, feels that the option put forward by Max Weber has become unthinkable nowadays.[73] One would even say that it is purely and simply social sciences surrender in front of a social phenomenon which raises serious problems of political cohesion in young African states and old industrialized nations alike and, worse still in Eastern Europe.

In other words, there is, however, no unanimity on the definition of *ethnicity or ethnic group*. But a consistency is emerging from the exclusive feature of the resulting essentialist or constructed identities. On this aspect, politically used ethnic identities operate, to quote Achille Mbembe, at a local scale, in *a setting...that makes it possible*

---


[71] For criticism of these theories, refer to: Carola Lentz (1994,1998), Philippe Poutignat et Jocelyne Streiff-Fenart (1998).

[72] Weber, Max: Economy and Society ed. by Guenther Roth et Claus Wittich, Bedminster Press, New York, 1968, p.395.

[73] Lentz, Carola: Die Konstruktion von Ethnizität. Eine politische Geschichte Nord-West Ghanas, 1870–1990. Köln: Rüdiger Köppe. P. 31 et 627.

*the destruction of all social links but the identity one. It is this dislike link that justifies a working relationship of unbundling whose…*ethnic conflicts are *violently expressed.*[74]

## Debates with Respect to Africa

Theoretical flange ways shaped by these approaches will, very much, influence the debates on ethnicity with respect to African societies. Here too, a general idea on the theory of ethnicity does not emerge from discussions and empirical case studies. Colonial ethnology has purposely and in an unhealthy manner opted for essentialist and biological conceptions. Africanists' criticism has relied extensively on the instrumentalist or constructivist approach type to challenge the essentialist views of tribalism and any other forms of ethnically derived social and political events in African states. In order to get out of this counterproductive controversy between the two approaches, what would be conveniently referred to as *the new African ethnology*, would opt for the historical perspective. The objective of this *new African ethnology* is not to deconstruct African ethnic groups. But it is trying, through empirical studies, to lay the foundation of another historiographical analysis of pre-colonial African societies in order to better highlight the unconventional character of issues resulting from the colonial ethnology and to stigmatize the postcolonial political exploitation of ethnicity in Africa,[75] which combined with the importation of Jacobin model of democracy put the entire continent in deadly conflicts around the central political power control in multi-ethnic states with only a few exceptions.

With reference to objective and subjective definition criteria of the ethnicity concept, one raises the question whether this concept has not only been a euphemism of the concepts *tribe, clan, race, community* and to which people have given negative connotations. For the sake of conceptual clarity, it would therefore be interesting to deter-

---

[74] Mbembe, Achille: Politique de l'inimitié, La Découverte, Paris 2016, p.52

[75] Carola Lentz used this method in his work on Dagara people in West Africa (1994, 1998) and on ethnicity in Ghana (2000). It should however be noted that pioneer development of this method are found in studies by Cheik Anta Diop (1954, 1959,1975,1981…) and Théophile Obenga (1973,1974, 1980…)

mine what makes the difference between ethnic group/ethnicity and the State/the Nation in order to grasp the complexity of the African continent.

## Related Concepts: Race, Clan/Tribe, Community and People

### *Ethnic Group and Race*

It must be said that the concept of race came into literature a little earlier than that of ethnicity. On the basis of the 17th and 18th centuries' racial theories, people were classified according to their skin color and the shape of their skull. Specific cultural and intellectual competences as well as levels of rationality in terms of historic production and civilization were prescribed and recognized in some specific races. For instance, Hegel out rightly excludes Africa and the Negro from his historic totality and concludes that: *What, in fact, characterizes Negroes is precisely that their consciousness has not reached the contemplation of any given solid objectivity… Africa is therefore an ahistorical, undeveloped world, entirely prisoner of the natural spirit and whose place is still at the threshold of the universal history.*[76] Here, cultural differences of races are immutable and originally determined. According to Hume, the superiority of the white race is part of the natural normality of the best course of action.[77] 19th century racial theories of Gobineau, of Chamberlain and social Darwinism are subsequently added to Hume's views. For instance, according to Gobineau, there is *"a native, original, settled and permanent inequality between diverse races."*[78] As stated by Achille Mbembe, the notion of race therefore operates by *…representing the other not as similar to oneself but as a genuinely threatening object that one has to protect him/herself from, break from or that should simply be destroyed…*[79]. It is also on the basis of

---

[76] In: Obenga, Théophile: Cheikh Anta Diop, Volney et le Sphinx. Presence Africaine, Khepera, 1996 p.21–22.

[77] In: Ditrich, Eckhard J.: Das Weltbild des Rassismus, Frankfurt, Cooperative Verlag 1991.

[78] In: Obenga, Théophile: op.cit. p.36.

[79] Mbembe, Achille: Critique de la raison nègre, La Découverte, Paris, 2013, p.23–24

these theories that a civilizing and humanitarian mission was sought for and assigned to imperialism and later to colonization. Under the influence of anthropologists, the physical and racial appearance of people later became pivotal for reading their cultural potentials and birth skills to produce knowledge and technology, in short, to produce a "civilization". The classification between human races is based on inferiority and superiority, dominated and dominant. Another unstated objective of racism theorists was the preservation of the purity of the so-called superior races. A mixture with inferior races would result in humanity decadence. A peaceful cohabitation between races is, therefore, almost impossible and this is why relationships among races can only be confrontational. Races are threatening to one another and are hence permanently in competition. Only superior and domineering races will survive the Darwin competition by completely destroying inferior races.

The term racism does not only refer to a hierarchical order between races in the debates, but also related to people who share the same culture and origin are not necessary prone to living well together. Balibar defines this variant of racism as: *"Racism which, at first sight, does not postulate the superiority of certain groups or peoples in relation to others but only the harmfulness of abolishing frontiers, the incompatibility of Lifestyle and traditions."*[80]

Even as the concept of race lost its notoriety in the scientific usage, it was closer to that of ethnicity under its fundamentalist prospects. Being less loaded, the concept *ethnic group,* became an *Ersatz* to that of race. Kenneth Little towards the end of 1950s noted that: *"some biologists and anthropologists prefer to speak about ethnic groups instead of race."*[81] The negative connotation of the concept of race must be avoided. The term ethnicity becomes a euphemism for race. But in practice, the designation of ethnic or racial groups always observes the principles of common cultures of origin. In Germany, the

---

[80] Balibar, Etienne: Is there a Neo-Racism, in Balibar/Wallerstein (Hg): Race, Nation, Class. Ambiguos Identities, London New York 1991. (pp.17–28), p.21.

[81] Little, Kenneth: Color and common sens: Fabian Society and Commonwealth Bureau 1958 p. 25

terms 'Schwarzafrikaner' or 'Neger' (Black, African, Negro) are used, at the first glance, to refer to group members whose skin color is black, regardless of whether they come from the USA, France, Mexico or even Cameroon, and even if from the cultural point of view they have nothing in common with other black people living in Germany. Here, there is a difference between ethnicity and race. While the term ethnicity refers to a group within a state, that of race refers to a large spatial coverage, and mostly, to group members' of defined geographical origins. With regard to Negro, that is the Black, Mbembe rightly observes: *Africa and the Negro – a co-generation relationship links these two notions. Speaking of one term, as a matter of fact, is mentioning the other. One gives to the other its enshrined value…all Africans are not Negros. Nevertheless, if Africa has a substance; and is a substance, it is the Negro that provides Africa with that substance – wherever he finds himself in the world.*[82] Everywhere in the world, the black race refers to Africa. One would equally say that the white race refers to Europe as the geographical identification of its origins; whether a white person is American, south-African, his/her geographical identification is the West. The yellow race would refer to the Asian continent, even if the cosmopolitan citizen, thus stigmatized, has nothing to do with geographical space here and there in a globalizing world characterized by unprecedented migratory flows. If the concept of ethnicity has replaced that of race in literature, it has equally inherited its negative connotation.

This negative connotation obliges Aimé Césaire to prefer the notion of *identity* to that of *ethnicity*.[83] According to Aimé Césaire, the notion of ethnicity entails *necessarily unpleasant connotations*. For him, ethnicity means *what is fundamental, the foundation that holds everything and on which everything can be built; the irreducible hard core; what provides a man, a culture, a civilization with its specific twist, its style, and its irreducible uniqueness.*[84] At first glance,

---

[82]  Mbembe, Achille: op.cit. p.65

[83]  Césaire, Aimé: Discours sur le colonialisme, suivi du Discours sur la Négritude, Présence Africaine, 2004, pp.78–92

[84]  Ibid: P.88–98

one would say that the poet has an essentialist and fundamentalist perception of the ethnicity concept. But at the time, he was already in a forward-looking manner in the current global dialectic (global/local); a concept that strives to grasp and make it perceptible the *sui generis* relationship that links the universal to the individuals; a kind of local rooting of cosmopolitanism. Just as the cosmopolitan citizen who is at the same time domestic and citizen of the world; the universal is nothing but the sum of diverse singularities. Using the concept of identity instead of ethnicity to talk about Negritude (Blackness) as a fight against *deculturation* and *acculturation*, the complexity of Césaire's thought takes shape when he declares: *It is neither about "intergrism" nor about fundamentalism, even less about a puerile navel-gazing...I would therefore say: obviously yes, no to unplugging, no...the universal yes....but not by negation, but as the deepening of our own singularity... it is admittedly about a re-rooting, but also about a fulfillment, an overtaking and about the conquest of a new and greater fraternity.*[85] Here, the search for a new identity; the sense of belonging to somewhere, to a community is the prerequisite; the fertile base of integration into the world in terms of participation into the universality.

### Ethnicity and Clan/Tribe

As far as the concept of Clan and Tribe is concerned, from its origins, it had a degrading and disparaging connotation. It has been used to refer to groups of colonized populations placed under the political and economic yoke and under the cultural domination of stronger groups. Fluer-Lobban & al. clearly stress this negative understanding of the concept *tribe/clan* when they show that the concept has been *"exclusively (used) in reference to subject and colonised peoples and in relation with racist stereotypes that have been part of an ideology which enabled ruling nations and classes to maintain their domination."*[86] The history of European imperialism shows us how western anthropologists have deliberately chosen to describe African socie-

---

[85]  Ibid: p.91–92

[86]  Fluer-Lobban, Caolyn/Lobban, Richard/Zangari, Linda: Tribes: A Socio-political Analysis, in Ufahamu, vol.7, No.1 1976 pp.143–165. p.160.

ties as primitive and barbarous, and this is for the sole purpose of refusing that they are States, People and Nations. In their opinion they are simply Tribes. We, therefore, have on the one hand societies, well organised into States, Nations (Europe) and on the other hand, societies that are yet to make history, which are given the disparaging designation of *tribes* (colonies). Due to its negative content, the concept of *tribe* is called into question in the scientific world and the term ethnicity is finally preferred to it. According to Fluer, Lobban & al, the term ethnicity de facto inherited all the negative connotations of the terms clan/tribe and especially its racist trends.[87]

*Ethnicity and Community*

The concept of *community* is as polysemous as that of *ethnicity*. In its broader sense, it refers to a social entity larger than ethnicity. It expanded fast with the Durkheim modernization process in which, the mechanical solidarity of the traditional society is replaced by the organic solidarity. It is no longer necessarily the blood relationship or the cultural origin or the sharing of the same history or the same language that connect individual to one another. It is neither the subjective belief in common interests that one has to defend in a competitive situation. Members' unity rests upon what they objectively share in common, such as short or long term values: professional or institutional anchor, social habitus (hobby), and religion. The sense of the same homeland (ethnicity) is one of such element but here, community is a euphemism to ethnicity or nation. When we talk of Jewish, Muslim or Christian community of Germany, France or Cameroon or of the Senegalese or American university community, it is about people who share the same religious belief or the same professional anchor regardless of their racial, ethnic belonging or nationality. But when we talk of the French community in Cameroon and vice-versa, of the Bulu community of Bafoussam, or the Mbouda community of Douala, we are also referring to people who claim their belonging to a land or a home depending on the relational scale, regardless of their religious belief or professional anchor.

---

[87] Fluer-Lobban & al.: op.cit. p.160

The concept of community thus proves to be superior or equal to that of ethnicity according to the social levels of appraisal.

*Ethnicity and People*

Right from its Romanic origins, the term people better expresses the idea of a cultural homogeneity and a mythical unity that members of a people would share. According to Diettrich and Radtke, the German Romanic philosopher Herber, has used the word 'Volksgeist' (people's spirit) as an abstract form to refer to all the cultural constructs of a people such as its practices, its language, its moral standards and all its literature as well as its artistic construct.[88] In the 19th century, biological criteria were also taken into consideration in defining the term *people*. As far as the term race is concerned, physical features are thus retained as identifying elements of different peoples. The cultural superiority and ability of a people are now judged by the dominance of its language in literature and poetry. Peoples are now classified according to categories of inferiority and dominance; primitiveness and civilization. Popular and populist adjectives become associated with aggressive and xenophobic ideologies such as Nazism in the German Reich under Hitler. With regard to its negative connotation, the term, *people,* was simply substituted in the literature by the term *ethnicity.*[89]

Kosellect, however, notices that through the different political regimes in Europe (from authoritarianism to democracy including institutional monarchy, parliamentarian republics and fascist regimes...), the term *people* plays a central role in the different social changes that have taken place in the 20th century.[90] In fact, the term until then negative, in the 18th and 19th centuries found itself progressively given a very positive connotation in terms of territorial sover-

---

[88]  Dittrich, Eckard J./Radtke, Frank-Olaf (Hg.): Ethnizität. Wissenschaft und Minderheiten, Opladen: Westdeutscher Verlag. 1990 p.21

[89]  Heckmann, Friedrich: Ethnische Minderheiten, Volk und Nation, Stuttgart, Enke Verlag. 1992, p.49

[90]  Koselleck, Reinhard: Volk, Nation, Nationalismus, Rasse, Kapitel XIV, in: Brunner/Conze/Koselleck (Hg.) Bd. 7, Geschichtliche Grundbegriffe, 1992, pp. 389–431. p.390

eignty of states and political power. The term, people, has become a constitutive element of the state and of the republic today. People are the sovereign owner of power, and it is through its suffrage that it can temporary delegate to any republican institution to use it. This constitutional understanding of the term people as a democratic strength was equally felt in the African continent from the 1990s. During the various processes of democratic opening imposed by the eastern wind in Africa, the term people has been exploited both by the political opposition and parties in power alike, and all has along shifted from its conceptual that created confusion with the term ethnic group. When in 1992, the *SDF* (Social Democratic Front) candidate turned the slogan power *to the people* into an electoral campaign slogan and the *CPDM (Cameroon People Democratic Movement)* introduced its candidate as *the people's choice* during the presidential elections of 2011, they were not referring here to an ethnic group, but rather to all the citizens of the Republic of Cameroon. In such a sociopolitical perspective, a clear distinction between the terms *ethnicity* and *people* is eminent with regard to the biologist and racist confusion of the 18th and 19th centuries. The term people thus became greater than ethnicity. The country's people include several ethnic and racial groups. Here, the main definitional features are no longer the cultural homogeneity and the mystical and mythical origins, but the sovereignty of the land of the country and the control of the central government whose legitimate owner is the people (all the citizens). And this is obviously within a democratic set-up.

However, it has been noticed that the exploitation of the term ethnicity in democracy raises the question of people's cohesion. Local politicians take advantage of these identities to claim resources within the state, and this is done on behalf of the group they think they represent. In so doing, they divide the people that make the state between *a **close relative** that could be opposed to a distant relative.*[91] Thus, the term natives who are at *home* opposed to *the others*,[92]

---

[91]  Mbembe, Achille: op.cit.(2016): p.58

[92]  Ibid.

which refer to ethno-regional origins of non-natives, becomes socio-political normalcy.

## The Need for a Conceptual Re-adjustment in the 21st Century

At this level of conceptual classification and taking into consideration the change of contexts, a re-adjustment of the perception of these concepts is necessary. Today, when one talks of the *Bantu People* in Africa or *Bamileke People* in Cameroon, it generates a conflict with the concept of *Cameroonian People*. The word *people,* is used nowadays to refer to all citizens of a country, who every day renew the plebiscite of their belonging to the nation related to the country concerned.[93] It is therefore practical to integrate these changes in perception into today's epistemological approaches and to rather talk of Bantu ethnicity, Bamileke ethnicity, Sawa ethnicity… which, in turn, is made up of Tribes such as *Bulu, Ewondo, Eton* or *Nda, Bafoussam, Bafang* or *Dschang, Mokon*… Bantu ethnic groups = *{Bulu, Ewondo, Eton…};* Bamileke = *{Mbouda, bafang, Dschang, Bangangte, Bafoussam…}*; Sawa= *{Douala, Bakweri…}*…These tribes are made up of clans (large families: *Essono, Atangana, Bell, Akwa, Bamendjo, Bamesso, Mokong, Mofo…*). If the term ethnic group incorporates the tribe, the latter is made up of several clans representing the various family strata.

In the final analysis, we can establish the difference between the term ethnic group as a group of people who objectively or subjectively think that they share the same inborn or constructed identity and the ethnicity, which is the phenomenon or the social fact of using or mobilizing the identity or the ethnic differences to benefit or discriminate against the included and the excluded in a competitive situation or sociopolitical cooperation in the sharing of resources. The management of these interactions between the included and the excluded has made a mark on the various political trajectories of the national unity processes in emerging African states in the years following independence and, today, continues to influence democratization

---

[93] It is in this context that we can talk of Cameroonian people, Senegalese people, French, German

processes on the continent since the collapse of the Berlin wall in 1989.

Another concept besides the term ethnicity in the heart of the analysis, which is also creating problems in the political integration process of emerging African states is the term *Nation*. This is why, it seems important to explain it according to different schools of thoughts and also see how this term, seen in the perception of the 21st century, is different from *Ethnicity*, a *People* and the *State*.

## What is a Nation in the 21st Century?

Like *Ethnicity*, the term *Nation* is highly controversial. If the term *Nation* has universally established itself in the history of political ideas as well as in the historic reality, it is however, not the case with its historical attributes from the synchronic and diachronic standpoints. Already in the European context where the term *Nation* derives its first political slogans, till date, there is no unanimity on the perception of the term *Nation*.[94] Since the French Revolution of 1789, a perception of the term Nation has been watchword in France drawing inspiration from father Sieyes concept of National Sovereignty which is fundamentally opposed to the vision prevailing in Germany and all of Eastern Europe. Marcel Prélot and Georges Lescuye rightly observed that with the liberal Father Sieyes, a Nation is made up of individuals enjoying full freedom and who are governed *by a unique power, subject to the same laws willingly created by them...the nation builds up with individual members who are legally independent.*[95] According to this model, a Nation is seen as a community of citizens governed by a constitution to which members freely accede. However, Sieyes finds his *Nation* in the third-state which embodies it. For him, the third-state, which is the European working class in full industrialization process, includes all what makes the *Nation* and everything that is not the third-state is, therefore, not part of the Nation.

---

[94]   There is a difference between Western Europe and Eastern Europe.

[95]   Prélot, Marcel/Lescuyer Georges: Histoire des idées politiques 13ᵉ Edition Dalloz 1997. p.359

Against this French model based on citizens and the fundamental law, the German model has the essential connotation of the concept of a *people*. Here, it is the blood relationship, language and culture that make a nation. This fundamental distinction between the previous French model and the recent German model deeply influences and guides scientific research on the phenomenon of *Nation*.

### The Objective Approach

According to Karl West Deutsch, a *Nation* is a *People* that own a State.[96] That is a people that enjoy land sovereignty and who are governed by a central political power. In Deutsch's writings, the element of blood relationship and the origin is evident in the connection *Nation* and *People*. He adds *communication* to the definition. People must communicate and understand one another on every subject, whatever the content even from a distance, one would even say between generations. Here, the fluidity of communication among People depends on the sharing of the same language, historic background and cultural heritage. If, besides that, such a People have a state apparatus thus enjoying a political power, then we can say with Deutsch that this group of people constitutes a *Nation*.

Deutsch's perception has its limitations. With Deutsch, one would not, for instance, talk of the nationalist movements in the various liberation struggles, given that these liberation struggles are prior to the existence of the states they fought for. One would, thus, talk about a German Nation only after German unity in 1871, which earmarked the creation of the Nation-State in Germany. Yet, way before this date, the Germans have long considered themselves in literature, poetry, the art and music as a fully-fledged Nation. There are people who consider themselves to be nations to the present day, but who are however, fighting unsuccessfully to create a their own state: the Basques and the Catalans in Spain, the Corsicans in France, the people of Tibet in China or the Kurds in Turkey or Iraq, the Sahrawi in Morocco etc. If we take the State as a pre-requisite for a nation or

---

[96] Deutsch, Karl W.: Nationenbildung – Nationalstaat – Integration. Westdeutscher Verlag, Wiesbaden. 1972 p. 202

vice-versa, then the number of sovereign States would be equal to the number of Nations.

With Weber, the existence of a State presupposes the common sharing of a strong and specific sense of solidarity between the members and this is in relation with outsiders. This shared sense of solidarity depends on the existence of other elements which are constituent parts of a Nation. It is, among many other things, culture, language, historical consciousness, standards and religion. These objectively identifiable elements are, to some extent, of particular importance in the formulation process of the national identity, which is the objective criterion for the distinction between members and non-members of the Nation.

In his endeavors to define the Nation, Stalin adds preceding criteria to the sharing of a common economic life that is communism.[97] Besides, the *common territory and common economic life criteria*, all other criteria of the objective approach are imposed to Nation members, and do not require, at all, their willingness to belong to the Nation or not. A common origin, same historical legacy, common language and culture are the main criteria that objectively build a Nation. This approach that defines the Nation with the so-called criteria which would be valid for all the Nations is not free from challenge. The Nation cannot be reduced to an immutable and natural phenomenon. Even the history of a people is not set in stones, it evolves, and this is why another traditional methodology in approaches to the definition of the concept of nation calls on various sociopolitical and historical factors.

### The Subjective Approach

The second theoretical framework which is relevant in defining the term Nation is the subjective approach. The ecclesiastic historian, Ernest Renan, reviewed and screened the objective definition criteria noted earlier. Taking into consideration the element of race as a national identity criterion, one realizes that European nations of the

---

[97] J.W. Stalin: Marxismus und nationale Frage. In: Werke. Bd.2: 1907–1913. Berlin 1950. p.272

time did not have any racial homogeneity. In France, as in England, the various contacts with the outside world led to irreversible blends of populations. This is also justified by the criterion of a *common language*. All speakers of English, Spanish or French did not and do not form, in any case today, a single Nation. This is a similar situation in Swiss where three population groups that speak different languages (German, French and Italian) live together as a nation. Besides some Arab countries where the Koran serves in the constitution with Islam as the state religion, religion is also not a basic defining criterion of a nation and several states have established secularism in their republican constitutions. Belonging to a religion is each citizen's individual freedom and therefore a private domain.

Renan, therefore, concludes that the life of a nation constitutes a domain of subjectivity. The life of a nation is spiritual and membership is determined by the individual will. According to him, a nation may be defined as a large solidarity community powerful enough for its members to clearly wish to live together. It is, thus, the wish to be a nation that creates a nation; it is the wish to be part of a nation expressed by an individual that makes him/her a member of that nation. Such a subjective perception of the nation stands out well in Renan's famous saying which states that the nation is *a daily plebiscite*.[98] The livelihood of a nation or belonging to a nation depends on the wish of wanting to live together and the sense of belonging. This is entirely at the discretion of the individual and not any historic, linguistic, racial, and religious or blood mythical heritage that would unite and link individuals to one another. A social aggregate only becomes a nation when members freely express the will to form a nation and organize themselves accordingly. In this subjective process, the emphasis is placed on the feeling or consciousness of the common will to form a political community that is in the modern sense of the term,

---

[98] Maus, Ingeborg: Vom Nationalstaat zum Globalstaat oder: der Niedergang der Demokratie in: Mathias Lutz-Bachmann/James Bohman (Hg.) Weltstaat oder Staatenwelt? Frankfurt am Main 2002. p. 232. *See:* Was ist eine Nation? Aus einem Vortrag des französischen Religionshistorikers Ernest Renan, gehalten in Paris am 11. 3. 1882 in Alter, Peter (Ed.): Nationalismus. Dokumente zur Geschichte und Gegenwart eines Phänomens. München 1994. pp. 45–47

a state, to which each member freely affiliates. In Renan's words, one will talk of a Nation of will or *Willnantion* (Willennation) according to Meinecke.

Contrary to Ernest Renan, Bernd Estel[99] understands by Nation, not only a political unity of individuals demonstrating the wish to live together but also sharing some historical and political legacy that enjoys a recognized sovereignty on a given land. With regard to the German Nation after the reunification, concurring to Bernd Estel's position, Habernas argues for the recognition of the constitution as the basic reference for the building of *a Staatsbürgernation* in Germany.[100]

It is the anti-Semitism that makes Renan's definition a hot topic. At the root of nation building, there is a series of contributing factors, risks, victories and in any case not necessarily natural or essential principle. The nation is, therefore, in Anderson's words, a sheer invention or fabrication.[101] At this level, the German historian Friedrich Meinecke's classification between what is called *Staatnation* (Nation-State) and *Kulturnation* (Cultural nation) is equally of particular importance in the theoretical perception of the concept of nation. The starting point of Meinecke's analysis remains the definitional features and criteria mentioned earlier. Related to the individual freedom and collective sovereignty, a Nation-state owes its existence to the will of the individual acceptance to belong or not to the nation. Here, we find Ernest Renan's approach again. In historical terms, countries like France and the United States of America are examples of a Nation-state. The nation is the embodiment of a conscious will of citizens who wish to live together in a well-defined land and under a central political power. The ethnic origin and the religious belief play no role in the process of belonging to a nation. The legal element that bestows the sense of belonging to a nation is not the com-

---

[99] Estel, Bernd, Das Prinzip Nation in modernen Gesellschaften. Länderdiagnosen und historische Perspektiven, Westdeutscher Verlag 1994

[100] Habermas, Jürgen: Der DM-Nationalismus in Die Zeit, 30. März 1990, n° 14, p.62

[101] Anderson, Benedict: Die Erfindung der Nation. Zur Karriere eines folgenreichen Konzepts, Frankfurt/M 1988.

mon language but the administrative and legal system, run by a central government. It should, however, be noted here that the difference between the two examples is that the USA is a nation created from a diverse ethnic basis, in which the ethnicity element is recognized and plays a political role; the French nation, indeed, was born from the individual will, but the ethnicity element was sacrificed and suppressed as a result of the unity of the French Great Nation.

With regard to the *Kulturnation*, the phenomenon does not depend on the existence of a State. Here, the nation does not need a state political institution to provide its citizens with the sense of belonging to the same national community. In historical terms, the nation predates the political institutions and the state. The individual will and freedom to belong to this community play no role. This perception of the nation was at the root of the emergence of communities in eastern and central Europe. The nation is seen as a natural community of fate to which the individual is predisposed at birth to belong. We can therefore make the connection between the objective theories of the definition of the term Nation and the *kulturnation* concept on the one hand, and the subjective theories of the State-Nation concept on the other hand.

Such a clear distinction between both theoretical approaches in defining the term Nation does not fit well into the political reality. In Switzerland, there are three large *kulturnation* with three different languages. But these three communities make a single Swiss Nation-State. A case where a common language is the legal element of the existence of a nation is France in which the mastery of the French language has become nowadays one of the criteria for granting of French nationality, when one clearly expresses the wish to belong. The French language is not only a tool of national pride, but a pillar of the French diplomacy as expressed in 1985 by Mitterrand in the following words:... *it is very significant, a private reserve that I claim when it has been trampled, it must be recaptured and given back to France. In this private reserve, I, first, see our language...We have remained in the heart of power relations. We still remain there, when we defend our language.*[102] In the final analysis, we therefore notice that beyond the single political wish to belong to a nation, factors such as language, culture and history play a great role in the process of nation building. For instance, the bottom line is that nationhood and patriotism towards a great nation result from the consciousness of historical, political and cultural events and legacy (Moliere, Descartes, Rousseau, Montesquieu, the French Republic, wars and victories, dynasties, the Eiffel Tower, the Champaign, French cheese,…) and not only the single expressed wish to belong to the French Nation.

Whatever the approach to a definition, the sense of belonging to a nation is referred to as national spirit, which in Realpolitik can hardly be separated from nationhood or patriotism. The intensity of this sense of belonging to a nation is called *national pride* and the intensity of national pride depends on the relationship between the individual and the nation, which, nowadays, is more determined by the role that the state plays in taking care of citizens' basic needs. If such a national sense or national pride goes along with a posture of aggression towards the members of another nation, we can then talk of nationalism in the negative sense of the term.

**Ethnicity and the Nation: two Operational Concepts**

Approaches to the definition of ethnic group/ethnicity concepts have shown that the term ethnic group often represents a group bound by a cultural and biological parent. In that sense, the term shares the same roots with the classificatory concepts of Race, People, and Tribe which in the European 18th century referred more to skin color, culture, tradition and community, origin, homogeneity, and which had acquired a negative connotation in the epistemological framework. In the essentialist prospects, the understanding of the term ethnic group is, thus, marked by the negative connotation of neighboring terms such as Race, People and Tribe. Owing to this second aspect, the use of ethnic group/ethnicity concept in politics runs the risk of perpetu-

---

[102] Kum'a Ndumbé III.: Was will Bonn in Afrika? Zur Afrikapolitik der Bundesrepublik Deutschland. Pfaffenweiler: Centaurus-Verl.-Ges.,1992 p.295

ating human beings' classification in fixed, unchangeable categories, objectively defined according to their biological and cultural parents, which operate in terms of inclusion or exclusion. It is this perception that has strongly characterized the first studies on ethnic group and ethnicity in African societies. With the advent of democratization processes, this natural vision of ethnic group was slightly qualified by the approach that perceives the phenomenon as a product of easily politically manipulated social constructions. Here, the ethnic group equally challenges the territoriality and is transposed to foreign spaces (diaspora) and even to the virtual world (social networks like Facebook, WhatsApp, and Twitter etc.) We are witnessing the age of the Virtual-Nation with no territory or a central power where communications tools (ICT) link members to each other.

Regarding the Nation, we equally noticed that there is no unanimity in the characteristics of the concept. Whether at the political level or in scientific debates, the perception of the term nation oscillates between two poles: the republican freedom to belong to a political construction and the natural determinism of a national identity inherited at birth. Gellner adds to the political concept of nation a basic ethnic legitimacy. Regarding the aggressive sense of national pride, he says: *"Nationalism is primarily a political principle, which holds that the political unit and the national unit should be congruent...in brief, nationalism is a theory of political legitimacy, which requires that ethnic boundaries should not cross political ones."[103]* Here, one would talk of Ethno-nation and consequentially, the citizen's wish to belong to the nation or not is no longer taken into account.

However, it is interesting to note that the nation building process needs a supreme political body that takes action leading to some homogeneity at several levels. The standardization of one or several official languages, the standardization of the legal and tax system, the regulation of the education system are all legal elements of a nation that can only be implemented and coordinated by a state. Even Ernest Renan's every day plebiscite needs a minimum consensual basis that would be the incentive for the expression of the wish to

---

[103] Gellner, Ernest: Nations and Nationalism, Oxford. Blackwell 1983. pp.1–2.

belong to a nation. This means that criteria, objective facts and moments of political subjectivity are not necessarily excluded in a nation building process. They are, in fact, complementary, and a strict separation between the subjective and objective approaches of the definition is more theoretical than operational. The important point in our analysis is to make a distinction between an Ethnic Group and a Nation.

Implicitly, in order to establish the distinction between an Ethnic Group and a Nation, we need to know which of the two concepts predates the other. Max Weber's[104] approach may clarify the matter. According to him, the Ethnic Group depends on the individual belief in blood parenthood. This moment of individual decision to belong to an Ethnic Group is, indeed, also found in Ernest Renan's Nation, but the wish to have a political body makes of the Nation a much greater entity than the Ethnic Group. The wish to belong to a Nation goes together with the passion to be part of an existent state or one still in progress. The Nation-State is therefore identical to Weber's Nation. The requirement of a state sovereignty is thus, one of the political elements of the distinction between the Ethnic Group and the Nation. Whether a state exists or not, does indeed not depend on one or the other, but they are politically linked to one another. Both concepts can even purposely be used in French and English to simultaneously refer to one another. The history of international relations demonstrates that the concept nation is more used to actually refer to states. We, therefore, have the League *of Nations* to refer to the international organization created by the states resulting from the First World War. And later in 1945, the defunct League of Nations gave way to the United Nations Organization. Here, we clearly talk of *Nations*, yet, they are the representatives of politically independent entities which are member states. It is, therefore, the organizations of states and not of nations in the populist and essentialist connotation of the European 18th and 19th centuries.

With regard to the political body that the state is, we may say, in comparison with other solidarity communities that the nation is

---

[104] Weber, Max: op.cit. pp. 219–222.

broader than the ethnic group. The Nation is politically more inclusive than the Ethnic Group. It is a political body superior to the Ethnic group. Several ethnic groups may be part of the same Nation and may belong in this effect, to a single State. This political ranking of the Nation and the Ethnic Group is equally influenced by the contemporary international law. It is reasonable that a people claim its self-determination (Southern Sudan, Western Sahara, Serbians, Croatians…) that a nation claims the creation of its own State (Palestine etc.). But when it is about ethnic groups, the language is less positive: one would negatively talk of ethnic conflicts and cleansing within a state where the issue of national integration, democratic participation and a fair sharing of wealth and resources is not yet a political normalcy. This clarification shows that the *Ethnic group* and the *Nation* are clearly distinctive operational concepts.

After the conceptual clarification between the Ethnic Group and the Nation, clarifying neighboring categories such as Clan, Tribe and People would help to better analyze and assess the problem of African States ruined by ethno-political conflicts in various nation building and democratization processes since the 1960s and 1990s. It is, therefore, fair to say that in nation building processes, the nation is politically more inclusive than the Ethnic group. A single Ethnic group may constitute a nation, but politically speaking, the nation may include several ethnic groups. The latter, with reference to African nations in progress, imposes two political choices: either the ethnic element, crushed by a centralized homogenization policy, totally disappears or it retains its specificities and becomes part of a greater nation that it shares with other ethnic groups. This conceptual clarification and up-date finally help us to understand and establish the following classification order and political and social ranking: **Family<Clan<Tribe<Ethnic Group<People<Nation/State**.[105]

In inclusive terms, we have the following:

---

[105] Clan and Tribe entities are inferior to Ethnic Group; the Ethnic Group is inferior to the concept of People, which in turn is inferior to the terms Nation and State.

**Nation/State** = {People, Ethnic Groups, Tribes, Clans, Families, Offspring};

**People**= {Ethnic Groups, Tribes, Clans, Families};

**Ethnic Group**= {Tribes, Clans, Families};

**Tribe**={Clans, Families};**Clan**= {Families, Offspring}

This ranking of the institutionalization process of social aggregates can be represented in the following inversed pyramid:

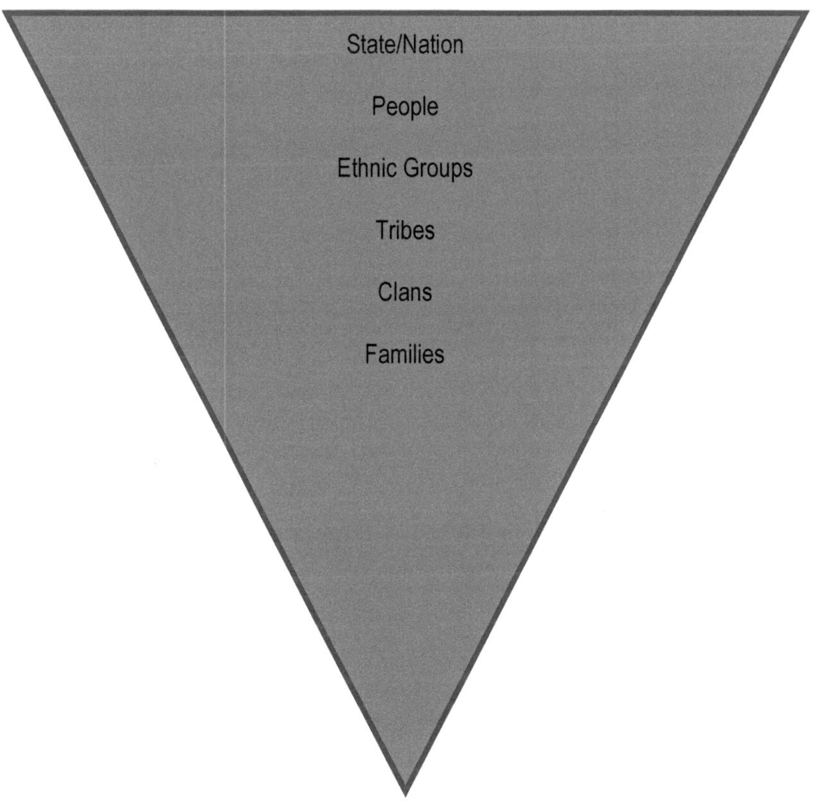


21$^{st}$ Century Institutionalization Process Pyramid of social aggregates

This conceptual clarity is a prerequisite for the formulation or reinvention of political options and new trustworthy constitutional mechanisms of governance that would include either in-born or constructed endogenous cultural realities of African societies while taking into account the new republican reality: democracy. It is a step towards an intelligible counterattack to the copy and paste model of *liberal democracy* and even *the Jacobin model* and also to the one-size fits all *Power Sharing* formulae. Hence, the second part of this study on the analysis of realpolitik in African States and the constitutional surroundings of the model of *Democratic Rotation in high office* not only as an alternative to liberal democracy, but also as a solution to pre and post electoral conflicts in African states torn between ethno-regional identities, national integration and democracies.

# CHAPTER 2

## Transcendence and Transformation of Ethno-regional Conflicts

In the first chapter of this analysis, the conceptual clarification of key terms and notions like *Ethnic Group, Nation* and related concepts (*tribe, race, community, people*), have been clearly defined in view of theirs methodologically operationalization. Their political and social articulations are at the heart of several cases of violence on the African continent. The question that this second part of the study seeks to address is clearly stated by Agbu Osita: *"Can ethnicity be reconciled with the struggles for citizenship rights and democracy within the unfinished nation-state project in Africa?"*[106] In other words, we would like to know to what extent, the phenomenon of ethnicity that has long been sacrificed on the altar of endless projects of nation building and national integration can be reconciled with the democratization and the establishment process of a sociopolitical order in Africa where human rights respect is a normalcy. Which political democratic mechanism can make this possible? So far, formulated and implemented responses have been carried out under political arrangements known either as ethno-federalism like in Ethiopia or power-sharing, with the distribution of key political positions based on ethno-national geopolitics, such as in Nigeria and Cameroon (regional balance) or else in formulating transition governments of national unity including the opposition or rebels in largely open governments following situations of conflict escalation such as in DRC, Kenya, Zimbabwe, Ivory Coast etc. These examples abundantly show that the state political organization and its institutions' *modus vivendi* is a determining factor in the management of challenges

---

[106] Agbu, Osita A.: Ethnicity and Democratisation in Africa, Challenges for politics and development. Discussion Paper 62. Nordiska Afrikainstitutet, Uppsala, 2011, p.7

from ethnicity with regard to the national project of democratization and even the construction of a nation per se.[107]

We plan to show the limitations of the copy and paste model of liberal democracy in African countries following the eastern wind and the political arrangement of power-sharing as a management method of ethno-political conflicts in Africa; and to put on the table of debate or even to test the rotation in high office democratic model that includes the ethnic element into the political game, not in terms of ethno-regional or geopolitical distribution of resources such as ministerial positions, chief executive officers of public and parastatal enterprises, but in terms of consciousness of political acceptance of ethnic diversities and possible participation of all citizens in power on the eligibility basis. Since 2006, we have proposed the Democratic Rotation in high office model for the prevention and management of ethno-political conflicts in African states which have strong ethnic identity and regional diversities. This new approach to the question of ethnicity/democracy link is finally illustrated in the light of some case studies in Cameroon and Ivory Coast. Whether this approach is transferable to other countries or not, it would require further studies and case-by-case adjustments as may be necessary. Before getting to the point, let us take a look at the current state of affairs.

## The New Democratic Orthodoxy

After noticing the failure of more than 30 years of Official Development Assistance (ODA), in 1990, the West thought that they have found in political monopartism, one of the reasons, if not the main reason, for the lack of economic take off that various development theories and strategies, conceived and implemented since the end of the second World War, were supposed to provide African countries with.[108] Since the early 1980s, neo-liberalists overtook constitutionalists and Keynes' followers with Structural Adjustment Plans (SAP)

---

[107]   Tagou, Célestin: op.cit. 2006, pp.198–202.

[108]   Tagou, Célestin: *Les théories et politiques globales de développement de Truman aux OMD* in Pondi, Jean-Emmanuel (sd.): Repenser le développement à partir de l'Afrique, Afredit, Yaoundé 2011, pp.23–53

and the Washington Consensus. The state has to give way to the *market place* and to private economic actors.[109] This resurgence of economic neoliberalism went hand in hand with the freedom of political life: Democratization. Free trade is impossible under a dictatorship in which, the judicial system, public affairs governance, respect of human rights are ruined by the peddling of corruption plague, impunity, patronage and political influence. In such a context where the financial, human, material and intellectual capital is not safe, neoliberalism cannot unfold easily. Thus, in all western circles and environments, a new orthodoxy is gaining ground: the so far predominant idea that under-developed countries were not ready for democracy is being replaced by the new belief that *"democratic good governance is not an outcome or consequence of development, as was the old orthodoxy, but a necessary condition for development..."[110]* In the 16th France-Africa Summit from 19 to 21 June in La Baule, François Mitterrand told Heads of States and African governments that democratization of political systems on the continent was the new conditionality for Official Development Assistance (ODA). Access to more ODA would be granted if there is more democracy, good governance and respect of human rights. Thus, democratic governments are rewarded and those who are trampling human rights would be punished as clearly stated by the British Foreign Affairs Secretary: *"In practical terms, it means that we ... will reward democratic governments ... we should penalize particularly bad cases of repression and abuse of human rights."[111]* Good governance and democracy are thus *put forward as basic factors for the success of economic policies and more generally for development levels of African countries.*[112] More than 25 years later, the success record of this equation: democracy first, then development is of mixed feelings. Whatever the case with the various outcomes per country, it seems to us that the debate

---

[109] Preston, P.W.: Development Theory, Backwell 2002; Rist, Gilbert: Le développement Histoire d'une croyance occidentale, Presse de Science Po. 1996

[110] Leftwich, Adrien: *On the Primacy of Politics in Development* in Leftwich, Adrien: op.cit. p.4

[111] Hurd, D.: *Promoting Good Government*. Crossbow, Autumn, 1990, pp.4–5

[112] Razafindrakoto, Mireille & al: Gouvernance et démocratie en Afrique: la population a son mot à dire in Afrique Contemporaine, N°220, 2006, p. 7

is no longer whether Africa needed democracy or not in order to be developed, but rather about *...the African people's ability and right to invent democracy like other peoples of the world.* [113] Jean Bayart's remarks in the early 1990s that what democracy has become on the continent still remains at the forefront, because *it is no longer about questioning the African people's ability to embrace foreign models of political organization... the matter now is to take strategic measures of inventing democracy, initiated by identifiable actors and compelled by the power balance...*[114] In the 1990s, this debate, neither from Africanists nor from the Africans themselves failed to bring a solution to any model tailored to African countries. Instead of bringing the proclaimed development, today, there is rather a multiplication and an exacerbation of intra-state conflicts (meso-conflicts) between ethno-regional groups in the shadow of political power conquest or monopolization by rebels or the opposition who are challenging election results (especially presidential elections); or by political regimes that cling on to power through electoral holdups, civil society intimidation and muzzling following forced changes of constitutions and electoral laws. One wonders why there is such a political regression on the continent. The answer to this question can be found in the mismatch of copied and imposed models of democracy models as the way out of political crisis.

## The Mismatch of the Western Model to Divided Societies

A glance at the African political history shows that what has happened on the continent in the last 25 years was merely an import of the Westminster and Jacobin democracy model: that is, a transposition to African societies of a democracy model developed and adequate to western societies such as France and England.[115] It is the

---

[113] Bayart, Jean François: *La problématique de la démocratie en Afrique noire « La Baule, et puis après ? »* in Politique Africaine N° 43, Octobre 1991. pp.11–17

[114] Ibid. p. 17

[115] For theoretical limitations of the Westminster model (majority democracy) refer to: Sisk, Timothy D.: Power Sharing and International Mediation in Ethnic conflicts, USIP Press, Washington, DC 2002 et Roeder, Philip G.& Rothchild, Donald (ed.) in: Sustainable Peace *Power and Democracy after Civil War*, Cornell University Press, Ithaca and London 2005

liberal and majority democracy. It does imply a political game that results in a polarization of the political scene between the democratic majority/majorities and minority/minorities. Here, the electoral game is at *"zero-sum politics"*[116] and the simple majority operates in terms of a majority inclusion and minority exclusion dichotomy. The majority wins it all and the minority loses it all; *"the losers get nothing"* to use Roeder and Rothschild's words.[117] Such a model operates in a context in which the political culture has reached a level where each citizen can freely make his/her political choices with no risk of any type of intimidation or retaliation. In such a context, a peaceful political alternation between partisan majorities and minorities based on demography can thus take place depending on options taken by the people through ballots. This, without any sort of complain from whomever about the domination and the marginalization of any group. In any other context than that of full citizenship development and partisan political consciousness, this model will, in the long run, lead to the frustration of the minority whose political survival is threatened. In a situation where the majority/minority criterion is not demographic but rather political and economic, that is a demographic minority becomes a political or economic majority,[118] then, this demographic minority uses all the necessary state resources to monopolize the political power and its economic influence in order to ensure its survival. This powerful minority has no interest in respecting the rules of the political game of the majority democracy. It therefore uses all means to keep the power including the democracy torpedo through the rigging of the electoral game with forced changes in its fundamental laws. Thus, the frustration goes over to the other side: it is the demographic majority that must either succumb to political patronage or shut up. But how long does this last? In any case, the system remains weak and one may conclude with Roeder and Roth-

---

[116]  Sisk, Timothy D.: op.cit. p.33

[117]  Roeder, Philip G.&Rothchild,Donald: op.cit. p.7

[118]  For the various nuances of perception of the conceptual dualism between the majority and the minority refer to Tagou, Celestin: « La typologie des minorités dans des sociétés plurielles » in Gwoda Adder & al. (sd.): Le Nord-Cameroun à l'épreuve des pluralismes, L'Harmattan, Paris, 2012 PP.35–49

schild that in a context of *"ethnically divided societies…majoritarian democracy does not protect minorities sufficiently….When majoritarian democracy becomes ethnically exclusive, the political system is less likely to be stable over long term – threatening the survival of both peace and democracy."*[119]

It is, thus, becoming clear that the 1990s copy and paste model is a permanent and everlasting source of conflicts between political actors in several African countries. If democracy simply refers to what Lincoln has described as *"the government of the people by the people and for the people"*[120] and given that there is no one-size fits all model, it is then a matter of strategy, structure and methodology; how one gets to power and how one leaves it, who determines the level of democracy of a political regime and consequently ensures good governance through the checks and balances mechanism that the holder of the sovereign authority has, that is the people. It is, therefore, not a universal model that would highlight the level of democracy in a given country. It should equally be noted that even after opting for the liberal democracy model, access modes and mechanisms to the supreme power in Germany (the Chancellery), in France (the Presidency), in England (the Prime Minister), and in the USA (the Presidency)…are different from one another.[121] These differences in regulating the political game in Germany, France, Great Britain and in the USA follow the consideration of the specificities of each country's sociocultural contexts and historic trajectories. However, they are all considered as old democracies, but with electoral mechanisms specific to each of them and, thus, adequate to different models. At some point the question of political engineering was

---

[119] Roeder, Philip G.&Rothchild,Donald: op.cit.p.7–8

[120] Abraham Lincoln: *The Gettysburg Address of November 19, 1863.*

[121] In Germany, federal parliamentarians elect the chancellor in the Bundestag; in France, the president is elected by a direct universal suffrage; in England, the constitutional monarchy goes hand in hand with liberal democracy; in the USA, in 2016, we noticed how democratic candidate Hilary Clinton had more than 3 million popular votes than the republican candidate Donald Trump. But the super voters made the difference to the benefit of the republican candidate, who, democratically speaking, had the minority of votes. They all respect universal principles and values of democracy, but with very different models adapted to their historical and socio-historical realities.

raised in all these societies described today in terms of old democracies. It is in this light that the question raised by Timothy Sisk is still at the forefront in African countries plagued with multifaceted violence: *"In deeply divided societies, which kinds of institutions and practices create an incentive structure for ethnic groups to mediate their differences through the legitimate institutions of common democratic state? ....how can the incentive system be structured to reward and reinforce political leaders who moderate on decisive ethnic themes and to persuade citizens to support moderation, bargaining, and reciprocity among ethnic groups?"*[122]

Today like yesterday, it has to be noted again that the partisan and individualistic conception of the notion of political power in the western sociocultural pedestal is diametrically opposed to the perception that has the same concept in the African sociocultural context. Under the influence of African customs and age-old ways of life, since the independence, an essentially community-based political power has built up. When one has nationwide power, it is not, in the first place individual power or that of one's political party. It is, above all, the power of one's community group or better still, the power of his/her ethnic group, because it is the loyalty and the fidelity of this ethnic group that give the power. It is thanks to this loyalty and fidelity that one was able to get the power and it is through the unconditional support of brothers and sisters of the ethnic group that one stays in power. It is thus, that in Cameroon for instance, under Ahidjo's regime, it was normal and it was a popular expression of grassroots approval that *"power belonged to the Northerners"*[123]just because President Ahidjo was from the northern Cameroon. Today the expression is: *"it is sad to say, but we have the power."*[124] President Paul Biya is certainly the only constitutional holder of the executive power, but with him, all the component communities of the anthropological group of the Pahouins of the Center, Eastern and

---

[122] Sisk, Timothy D.: op.cit. p.33

[123] Mbuyinga, Elenga: Tribalisme et problème national en Afrique Noire. Le cas du Kamerun, L'Harmattan 1989, p.76

[124] Ibid.: p.86

Southern Cameroon feel that they have the power. This perception of power is equally noticeable at the level of simple members of the government. Here one is first the minister of his/her ethnic group before being at the service of the Nation. About Cameroon, Nyamjoh has the following remarks: *"The same is true of ministers whose first visits after appointment are usually to their home village to muster support and /or gratitude for the center, as well as to prove that they have a power base of some sort. This also reveals that they are first and foremost ministers for their ethnic group, before being ministers for Cameroon as whole, if at all."*[125] Tadadjeu echoes in the same light: *An unwritten but very powerful political principle in Cameroon requires that when someone from a province or from a group of provinces with some common features is in power, all the people from this province or region are implicitly in power… natives of this region will have the lion's share in the national cake. In other words, they will eat more than others.*[126] Whether right or wrong, each member of this group feels that he/she has the power and will do everything to monopolize it, and consequently has to prevent any possibility of political alternation. Here the elitist political patronage between the center and the peripheries is operational. In such a context, liberal democracy in terms of free *individual eligibility* through political parties proves to be incompatible. Here again, the citizen has the tendency of making political choices justified more by the belonging to a community (tribe, ethnic group) than a deep and firm belief in a partisan and programmatic option inspired by political platforms.[127]

This difficulty masks another which is basic in the *Weltanschauung* of different peoples. The liberal and majority democracy model that the West is trying to impose to African societies falls within a power

---

[125] Nyamnjoh, Francis: Cameroon: A country united by ethnic ambition and difference, in *African Affairs*, (1999), p.109

[126] Tadadjeu, Maurice: Démocratie de Partage du Pouvoir; Pour le modèle P3 au Cameroun. Edition BUMA KOR, Yaoundé 1997. P.40.

[127] Case studies carried out on Cameroon on this topic are quite instructive. Refer to Menthong, Helène-Laure: Vote et communautarisme au Cameroun: un vote de cœur, de sang et de raison, in *Politique Africaine* (1998) 69, p.40–53 ; Nyambjoh, Francis/Rowlands, Mechale: Elite Associations and the politics of Belonging in Cameroun, in *African Affairs*, (1998) 68,3, p.320–337

perception that is at the same time partisan and individualist. Here, social changes resulting from the modernization process through the industrialization and rationalization of the production circuit and mechanisms have given rise to an excessive individualization of social relationships. It is in this vein that Durkheim has observed the fact that the *mechanic solidarity* of the traditional society has been replaced by the organic solidarity in which interest and the utilitarianism are at the heart of relationships between social aggregates.[128] With these changes, the power is also perceived differently. What matters here, are individual aspirations and partisan ideals. It is the corporatist networking that determines the individual socialization and no longer the blood link or the relationship with his/her home community.

While in African societies one observes an urban socialization that builds its base on ethno-geographical origins, which consequently creates a much more community political perception of the power as mentioned earlier by Nyamnjoh and Tadadjeu[129]. In western societies one can rather observe an excessive social rehabilitation. It is therefore, quite normal and socio-politically acceptable that in Cameroon, for instance, a political party militant has to return HOME, that is his/her region, to his/her home village and more precisely where his/her parents come from to be eligible for a council advisor, mayor, member of parliament or a senator position even when he/she resides, works and pays taxes in another village, another town, another region of the same country, but where he/she is considered non-native.[130] This socio-political logic accepted by each and every one simply describes a perception of power that does not go hand in hand with the liberal democracy model that underpins the individual free-

---

[128] Giddens, A: Emile Durkheim Selected Writings, Cambridge University Press, 1972a, ibid.: Capitalism and Modern Social Theory, Cambridge University Press, 1971; Lukes, S.: Emile Durkheim, London, Macmillan, 1973

[129] Nyamnjoh, Francis et Tadadjeu, Maurice op.cit.

[130] In Cameroon political history, it is worth to note and to congratulate natives and non-natives a few exceptions such as Mr. Paul Eric Djomgoué, Mr. Fampou Dagobert late Mrs. Foning Françoise who respectively had been and are Foundi Division parliamentarian, mayors of Douala while they are native of the West region.

dom to take part in elections everywhere within one's home country. In addition, ethno-exclusive concepts of native, non-native or foreign-born[131] that have become necessary in African sociolinguistics following the examples of Cameroon and Ivory Coast, where their exploitation in politics has reached worrying dimensions, are true indicators that demonstrate that African countries are still far away from republics in which citizens freely exercise their rights and civic duties everywhere. Between the lines, it becomes clear that the social fact is obstinate: the existence and the respect of citizens' home community and ethnic group in African countries with strong ethno-regional diversity are identity elements with a real sociopolitical weight, but that contemporary actors hypocritically strive to ignore. And still, they seek and use it in all sectors of civil service and at all levels of political life, when one comes to reallocation of resources.

It must be said that this rejection of the majority democracy is not synonymous with the dismissal of the values and cardinal principles of democracy per se. Having recognized its incompatibility with divided societies, theoretically and in reality, an alternative was quickly found in the Power Sharing model. The sharing of power has not only become the cornerstone of all international mediation missions in contexts where violence occurs, but also the pragmatic pedestal of *national union* government platforms or broad-based *national consensus* here and there on the continent. Thus, we may raise the question whether Power Sharing, can address the shortcomings of liberal and majority democracy in divided societies.

## Power Sharing

Of Anglo-Saxon origin, the concept *Power Sharing* in French language literally means *partage du pouvoir* (the Sharing of Power). According to Rothchild and Roeder,[132] the introduction of the con-

---

[131] In Ivory Coast, the concept of native is used to refer to a native that had had access to a land title in a place that is not his/her origin. In this case, access to a piece of land still does not give way to community integration. You remain a non-native.

[132] Rothchild, Donald &al.: "Power Sharing as an Impediment to Peace and Democracy" in Rothchild, Donald &al.(ed.): Sustainable Peace Power and Democracy after Civil Wars, Cornell University Press, Ithaca and London, 2005, p.30

cept into the English language dates back around the 1970s with the Sunningdale Agreement of November 21st 1974 in Northern Ireland between Unionists and Social-democrats. In fact, resulting from the disputed elections of June 28th, 1973, the formation of local government of January 1974 was possible thanks to this agreement that shared the power between the unionist majority and Irish nationalist minority. At the research level, Works of Arend Lijphart (1968, 1977), of Eric Nordlinger (1972) and of Donald Horowitz (1985) are among the first studies whose analysis centered on the functioning of democracy in divided or plural societies.[133] But in 1965, Arthur Lewis, already raised the issue of a type of democracy specific to developing countries with respect to the weak political culture of the population and actors in the political arena. He then talked of consociational democracy.[134] It is a political and institutional arrangement that proportionally and consensually shares political resources at the decision-making between socio-cultural components of a given country.

Power sharing is, thus, organized in Realpolitik through what is called the formation of broad national consensus or national union based governments. In such governments, warring parties of intrastate conflict or the demographic or sociocultural components within a state are represented. In addition, the quota system is practiced in sharing parliamentarian positions, decision-making positions, and finally, options such as Affirmative Action, Regional Balance (a kind

---

[133] Horowitz, Donald L: Ethnic Groups in Conflict. University of California Press, Berkeley, 1985; "Making Moderation Pay/ Comparative Politics of Ethnic Conflict Management" in: Montville, Joseph V(ed.).: Conflict and Peacemaking in Multiethnic Societies, Lexington Books, New York, 1991 (451–475); Lijphart, Arend: The politics of Accommodation: Pluralism and Democracy in the Netherlands. University of California Press, Berkeley, 1968; Democracy in Plural Societies: A Comparative Exploration. Yale University Press, new Haven, 1977; Power Sharing in South Africa: Policy papers in International Affairs. University of California Press, Berkeley, 1985; "The Power-Sharing Approach" in: Montville, Joseph V. (e.) op.cit. Conflict and Peacemaking in Multiethnic Societes, Lexington, 1990b (491–510) et Nordlinger, Eric: Conflict Regulation in Divided Societies, Center for International Affairs, Harvard University, 1972

[134] Lewis, W. Arthur: Politics in West Africa, London 1965 in Allen, Goerge &al.: The consequences of Negociated Settlements in Civil Wars 145–1993, American Political Science Review 89: 681–690

of positive segregation) are used aiming at the development of an elite in social groups or intellectually or economically backward regions or people who are politically or administratively under represented at the national level, not to mention the underprivileged ones.

That is how at the international relations level, power sharing has benefited from a renewed interest in several post-cold war conflict resolution processes. It has become the conceptual basis of peace agreements for resolving political and military crisis since the 1990s, and has served as a basis for the restoration of negative peace following several political conflicts and crises on the African continent. We have the Arusha peace agreement in 1993 for Rwanda; the Sun City for DRC in 2002; the Naivasha between 2003 and 2004 for Sudan or the Ouagadougou in 2007 for the Ivorian crisis. Quite rightly, Rothschild and Roder think that: "...*power sharing has become the international community's preferred remedy for building peace and democracy after civil wars.*"[135] It has become a kind of answer to everything to international mediators in various intra-state conflicts in Africa and Eastern Europe alike at the end of the East-West ideological confrontation. Most conflicts are ethno-regional and the international community has used power sharing to introduce an arrangement between the warring parties with the representation of each ethno-regional group in transitional governments, in parliaments or in decision-making political sectors that affect the life of the nation.

### *Power Sharing Approaches*

There are two main approaches of theoretical and practical approaches of power sharing in the literature: the *consociational* approach and the *integrative* approach.[136]

---

[135] Rothchild, Donald &al.: "Dilemmas of state-Building in Divided Societies" in Rothchild, Donald &al.(ed.): Sustainable Peace Power and Democracy after Civil Wars, Cornell University Press, Ithaca and London, 2005, p.5

[136] The established English notion is that of "consociational approach" whose basic concept is "Consociationalism" (Arendt, Lijphart, 1968) which introduces the concept of political accommodation or arrangement before his 1977 book (Democracy in plural society) On the fundamentals of the Consociationalism concept (Nordlinger op. cit ; Sisk Timothy D. op.cit). Jurg Steiner's 1974work on Switzerland and 1981 articles: The

*In the consociational approach,* collaboration between political elites is the cornerstone in the management of ethno-regional conflicts in a given country. Ethno-regional diversities, discrepancies and interests are managed by a kind of cooperation between legitimate or social-network based representatives of ethnic groups. Presumably, the political elite understand the stakes better than the masses and cooperate intelligently between each other to ensure a social and political coexistence between their various groups. Thus, building peace even if, it is negative peace. Arend Lijphart pointed out four fundamental principles for the success of what he calls "consociational democracy":

- a large parliamentary coalition to manage the legislative power;

- a mutual veto power to warrant the consideration of interest especially of minorities in relation to the majority;

- a proportionality principle at all levels of decision-making in government, public administration, justice and big parastatal firms;

- some degree of autonomy in the administrative management at the local level in the form of federalism or decentralization.

He equally adds a few necessary conditions among which masses loyalty in relation to the elite; a balance of power between groups; the size of the country; the existence of moderate elite and inter-community identity markers. This is how he believes that for non-western plural societies there is no choice between British majority democratic model and consociational democracy, but rather between the latter or no democracy at all.

This approach has given rise to quite a number of reservations including the ones from Sisk and Horowitz:

---

consociational Theory and Beyond » Comparative POLITICS 13 (April), 348–351 et « Research Strategies Beyong Consociational Theory », Journal of politics (Novembre) 1241–1250 amply contributed to feed the controversy around the concept.

- Confidence in the elite has its flip side in the sense that they can cleverly initiate or stage-manage ethnic conflicts or tensions for individual purposes and nurture political patronage between them at the expense of the real interests of the masses that they pretend to represent at the national level. Here the elite exploit the ethnicity for their selfish interests.

- It also runs the risk of crystallizing Barth's ethnic *boundaries*[137] and considering vital identities constructed from scratch by the elite to maintain and justify pseudo-regional claims in politics. There is, therefore, no guarantee that the elite will use their position to reduce interethnic tensions.

- The mutual veto power reduces democracy per se to nil and paralyses the process of political decision-making

- This approach relies on the constraint of the elite to make arrangements between them and not on the democratic will of the masses that is the people. And in the best case, the people's ability to divorce from the elite and initiate and take responsibility by themselves for popular movements of protest is equally neglected.

With regard to the reservations on the consociational approach, Horowitz[138] has defined a typology of the second approach to Power Sharing which is intended to be integrative via five mechanisms that, according to him would resolve ethno-regional conflicts in diverse societies. These are the following:

- Territorial dispersion of power between the center and the periphery. This can be captured in the wish to reduce the potential threat that a single group may accumulate;

---

[137] Barth, Fredrik: op.cit.

[138] Horowitz, Donald: Ethnic Groups in Conflict. Berkeley, University of California Press, 1985

- Fostering competition between the elite at the local level which could lead to supra-ethnic votes to be part of the large coalition at the national level;

- Promotion of social clusters, inter-grouping for the development of mixed or metis identities.

Federalism or power decentralization and the importance given to the proportionality and the checks and balances between groups seem to be the common factors to the two approaches of Power Sharing. However, when the political game is controlled in such a way that the elite obligatorily need the political support of super-grouping votes, the interethnic cooperation becomes a must in the integrative approach. Secondly, relegating the elite legitimacy to the people through elections, puts out of the way radical leaders and rewards moderate actors politically. This provides a bottom-up sociopolitical anchoring in the moderation between elite and resolves the consociational top-down approach. In this context, leaders are more likely to make concessions at the national level or at the center which better stabilizes and democratizes the political system in a divided society. Minorities are no longer simply represented but do have a real influence. Donald Horowitz describes three institutions and political practices that make effective the integrative approach.[139]

- *Federalism:* conscious of the fact that Federalism may exacerbate ethnic conflicts and lead to secessionist tendencies, Horowitz sees the great importance of federate states as real regional arenas that train leaders in a political culture of concessions and coalitions for a greater political game at the national level. In doing so, federalism reduces conflicts at the national level relegating several questions to the regional level. There is an additional advantage of developing several political parties, thus reducing the risk that a single party has a grip on the whole country.

---

[139] Horowitz, Donald: op.cit. and Sisk, Thimothy: op.cit. p.34–45

– *The electoral system* must induce a fragmentation of the popular support that a candidate needs to be elected. The alternative voting system requires that candidates create multiethnic electoral lists in order to gain a second or third voice from voters who are not part of their natural electoral basis. In order to gain these interethnic alternative votes, candidates must be moderate and ready to make concessions in their political options in relation to the interests of all the socio-ethnic components of the country. While putting into context the importance of the electoral system in a fragmented society, one understands once more why the liberal majority model of democracy is creating problems in Africa with regard to what has happened in DRC, Kenya, Ivory Coast and in Gabon during the last elections.

– *The presidential system:* in the integrative approach a president elected by a direct universal suffrage by absolute majority represents the will of members of several ethnic groups in a plural society. In order to have such a majority, a leader must demonstrate political moderation, concessions and conciliation in political stakes that affect the interests of all the groups and thus, the relocation policies of resources reduces socioeconomic inequalities and injustice between groups. These predispositions provide him/her with the posture of a statesman devoted to unity and nation building.

In this integrative approach, the political culture has given birth to political voters and elite fully enfranchised from ethno-regional heaviness. Indeed, there are still some radical and ethnocentric political voters and elite, but moderate ones constitute a democratic majority which is the basis for the political integration of all groups at the national level. No extremist political position is fortunate at the national level. It is in this setup that the strongest version of the law of *median voter* by Black Duncan is best articulated.[140] That is, the voter who prefers the median political opinion to the extremes in the

---

[140] Black, Duncan: On the Rationale of Group Decision-making in *Journal of Political Economy,* 56(1) (1948): pp.23–34.

majority. Avoiding being extremist or radical, the politician, there-fore, plays on this position for his/her election. It was the case in the Federal Republic of Germany where Chancellor Angela Merkel's Christian Democrat party used the *"Politik der Mitte"*[141] as its motto in the 2001 campaign to take the chancellery from the Social-Democrat Gerhard Schröder. Any too far right or too far left politics had no chance of bringing together the German majority. In the same vein, the success of the *"En Marche"* movement of French president Emmanuel Macron in the 2017 presidential elections is understanda-ble. With this movement he freed himself from the traditional politi-cal division between the far left, the left, the right and the far right of the French political landscape: *En Marche is an open movement to everyone without exception.*[142] It is a movement in which the median voters find themselves and form the majority.

It is actually noticeable with regard to Africa that the majority of countries opted for an integrative approach in a presidential system that has become the drift of all political abuses. Here, the median voter does not yet exist. Voting has an ethno-regional basis. The root of a democracy model specific to our societies is therefore in its law or electoral system for access to high office, which is the presidency of the Republic.

Sisk has noted that the entire arsenal of arguments from Horowitz's integrative approach of power sharing lacks case studies in which there are all the above mentioned mechanisms and institutions. He then concludes that the basic difference between the two approaches lies in the way a multiethnic coalition is formed and its nature. In the consociational approach, the political coalition at the center is formed after elections, and when the elite cleverly take note that any exclusion policy would be counterproductive for the entire society. In the integrative approach, coalitions are formed before elections in order to bring together multiethnic votes.

---

[141]  http://www.faz.net/aktuell/politik/cdu-csu-merkel-plaediert-fuer-politik-der-mitte-124264.html.Consulted on 12/10/2017

[142]  https://en-marche.fr/ Consulted on12/10/2017 à 19h06

*Power Sharing as Conflicts' Management Tool*

It is hard to have a clear-cut stance on which of both approaches to power sharing is the most suitable choice for conflict management in all ethno-regional diverse situations. Either approach has strengths and limitations depending on contexts. This is why, following Nordlinger, Sisk has made the effort to propose several options that form a menu from which peacemakers and mediators can draw appropriate solutions to the challenges of the ethnic conflict confronting them.[143] First, he defines three implementation domains or levels of power sharing in a given society, namely: **the territorial division of power** (*federalism, decentralization or Unitarianism*), **the decision-making process and mechanism** (*at the executive, legislative, administrative levels; the electoral system*) and finally **the State/Ethnic Group relationship** (*nature of political and public management of resources between the state entity or the Republic and ethno-regional diversities*). The variables of this analysis show verifiable indicators either in the consociational or integrative approaches.

- **Territorial division of power:** here the consociational approach proposes federalism where federate states have large management autonomy in several domains of political and socioeconomic life. While the integrative approach is for a unitary state which may ultimately proceed to the decentralization parts of decision-making according to the principle of administrative subsidiarity.

- **Decision-making process and mechanism:** the consociational approach follows a proportional representation and permanently seeks a consensus in taking big decisions at the executive, legislative and administrative levels. Here, proportionality is the appropriate electoral system. For the integrative approach, the decision-making process at the three levels (executive, legislative and administrative) follows the

---

[143] Here, the authors study only one type of conflict according to Galtung's typology: meso-conflicts this means conflicts between social aggregates within the same country.

majority principle, whether it is absolute or simple. There is a mixed electoral system between semi-majority and semi-proportionality.

- **State/Ethnic Group relationship:** Ethnic groups' rights are recognized in the consociational approach and any public policy takes them into account in the distribution of resources. At the integrative level, the consideration of groups is excluded from any public policy on behalf of the unitary state and the *one and indivisible Nation.*

Of all possible combinations of integrative or consociational indicators, it is clear that Power Sharing is put forward here as a real conflict management mechanism in plural societies where national consciousness and the political culture are yet to be fully developed. This is why some approaches of power sharing have often been put into practice in transition processes which are true moments of hope or jeopardy. In order to avoid the worst in a war situation where, no party really has an edge in the military field,[144] leaders who are fully aware are quick to negotiate or to accept a mediation in order to sign peace agreements to put an end to the suffering of the people that they represent while preserving some advantages and without losing face. The signature of a peace agreement seals the power sharing between the warring parties. It is the same for evolving societies where there might be a sudden and undemocratic change of the political system, the political regime and social governance. Here, leaders of protest movements or rebels and those of the government in place moderate their ambitions and make concessions while sharing resources mostly at the political and economic levels. The formation of national unity and/or transitional governments is the most visible demonstration of the power sharing policy as a conflict management mechanism.

---

[144] In a civil war situation resulting in a unilateral military victory, power sharing is not welcome. The regime would certainly look more stable and may often record a significant economic record, but this is often an imposed negative stability that stifles individual freedom.

In this respect, the Power Sharing approach may be understood as a transitory solution for the intra-state meso-conflict following a post-electoral political crisis between the party in power and the opposition or following a civil war opposing the government and rebels. In most cases, parties in conflict have an ethno-regional demographic basis and coloration. In the peace agreement resulting from power sharing, parties in conflicts accept a redistribution of resources; generally ministerial positions in a large national unity transitional government for a set period, at the end of which, elections will take place under the supervision of the international community. This is how Power Sharing has become one of the tools and one of the political outcomes that the international community (UN and other sub-regional mediators …) uses to bring about agreements between parties in ethno-regional conflicts. Hence, the relevant remark from Sisk is that: *"Power Sharing usually flows from a history of violent conflict or as an attempt to pre-empt the degeneration of intergroup relations into violence. In many contemporary instances, the international community….has intervened in civil wars and advocated power-sharing practices as part of the political component of broader efforts to manage the many facets of the complex emergencies spawned by these conflicts. Power-sharing outcomes…are the result of many of these interventions."[145]* An Evaluation of the outcomes of this conflict resolution mechanism brings out successes and shortcomings. Power Sharing has helped to bring about Negative Peace but has failed in building Positive Peace as indicated by David Barash.[146]

### *The Shortcomings of Power Sharing*

If with this approach the international community has been able to bring conflicting parties to sign peace agreements here and there in Africa, that is, leading them to reach a situation of Negative Peace, findings on difficulties linked to the application of power sharing during transitional governments, are quite obvious. This has been the

---

[145]  Sisk, Timothy D.: op.cit. p.87–88

[146]  Barash, David P: Introduction to Peace Studies WPC, 1991 p.299, p.459

case in Rwanda and Somalia conflicts in the 1990s and DRC, Kenya, Ivory Coast, Sudan and CAR conflicts in the 2000s. The main objective of these peace agreements, on the basis of power sharing has been the establishment of democratic governance at the end of the transition periods. However, elections related to these peace agreements have never taken place peacefully. They have neither not led to results accepted by all parties. Even in situations of no war as in Gabon, Kenya, the power sharing raises more national cohesion problems and brings about new socio-political challenges whose security and geostrategic stakes at the national and sub-regional levels are worrisome. From their organization to the proclamation of results, these elections have been enameled with uprisings and brutal repressions with their own set of mass killings and destruction of public and private property.

### *An Anti-democratic Short-cut*

The inconsistency with regard to democracy in Africa becomes blatant with post-electoral crisis or post rebellion exit methods. Here, power sharing between protestors, rebels and the power in place is easily appealed. This solution is subject to several limitations and, in the final analysis, proves to be more detrimental to the democratic process and the construction of Positive Peace than one could imagine. In order to be associated with a government, to be at the helm of power, it is no longer necessary to get the people's vote. Either you create an armed rebellion that takes a region of the country hostage, or challenge elections' results or else refuse to organize elections at the end of your turn in office with the single goal of taking over or maintaining power and, if necessary provoke a cycle of negotiation and mediation under the auspices of the international community, which advocates a single outcome: power sharing through a peace or political agreement. This is how, between 1990 and 2016 we have had power sharing in Rwanda, Somalia, DRC, Kenya, Zimbabwe, Ivory Coast and Southern-Sudan. The current example of the DRC remake calls our attention in a number of ways. The political elite in DRC is demonstrating once more how one can maintain himself in power at the end of constitutional constituencies by refusing to organize elections in time and stage-manage a national dialogue with an international community mediator whose single outcome is summarized in a new concept of *Glissement politique* (the sliding or the shifting of electoral calendar).[147] This is, once more thanks to power sharing between the president who remains in power and the opposition which is getting into power in the most anti-constitutional and antidemocratic manner. The observation that can be made is, that upstream or downstream, Power Sharing is everything but not democratic. It is a politically pragmatic arrangement to establish a Negative Peace at the expense of democracy and the rule of law in a Republic. Post-electoral conflicts resulting from manipulations and challenges of election results between 2010 and 2016 adequately demonstrate that in this context, the liberal and majority democracy model and the related electoral systems are not suitable. There is need for something else to transcend and transform endogenous realities for the development of a society where political change and participation are a normalcy. This other thing is a democracy model that takes into account current endogenous realities without destroying universal values and principles of democracy per se; whether these realities are constructed or not, a political mechanism must be built for the management of products of social constructions while waiting for the development of new constructions.

---

[147] In 2016, political science terminology acquired a new concept born on the left bank of the big Congo River. The concept of *"Glissement"* *(*the *shift)* which refers here to a series of political maneuvers cleverly put in place to avoid constitutional provisions regulating the limit of the presidential term in office and the organization of related elections within the set deadlines and this with the sole purpose of remaining in power. If all goes well, it is in 2018 that President Joseph Kabila will hand over the power to his successor having, thus spent two more years in power thanks to the *"Glissement"* policy. On the 8th of August 2018, the last day of deposit of candidacy for the December presidential elections, President Joseph Kabila has stepped down from his unacceptable ambition of running in for a third term. The Permanent Secretary of PPRD and former Minister of Interior, Mr. Emmanuel Ramazani Shadari is the awaited candidate of President Kabila political coalition. We hope Kabila will be fair enough and will to try to manipulate the upcoming elections or to implement a short of Poutinisation of political outcome in the DRC if Ramazani wins the elections democratically. Poutinisation refers to the politic of bypass between Vladimir Poutine and Dmitri Medvedev in Russia since 2005.

### *After Sharing the Cake, What about the Cherry?*

It is understandable that in some sociopolitical diversity contexts, where animosity has reached a point of no return and has neither been transcended nor transformed, a policy of participatory dosing in the management of public affairs is essential in order to avoid groups and regions' exclusion in the global development process of a nation. We salute approaches such as *Affirmative Action, Regional Balance*, but in several cases the logic of Power Sharing does not go all the way. It takes care of peripheral resources and remains silent about the central resource, which is not only one of the most important, and which, on the other hand is in itself the purpose of most ethno-regional conflicts that have existed and still exist in the continent today: **the Presidency of the Republic, the High Office.**Who will be the future **Father of the Nation?** Power Sharing has shown how to share other resources such as ministerial positions, CEO of large firms, but has failed to tell us how to share the seat of the President of the Republic. Yet, this seat is the main issue in several past and current ethno-regional conflicts on the continent. Given that sharing this seat is practically impossible, it is believed that democratic change would resolve the problem. Democratic change is unfortunately impossible with the fear of strategic groups (sometimes demographic minorities) of democratically losing the power for good and the frustration of conflicting groups (sometimes democratic majorities).[148] Those who are afraid of losing the Presidency of the Republic position for good and activate all political tricks to monopolize the power; while those on the periphery are getting busy to take power, or at worst to destabilize the country.

### *A Suspicious Coalition, Exclusive Political Outcome*

In addition to becoming an antidemocratic political bridge, Power Sharing proves to be apolitical incubator of governance negotiation. In different governments of national unity or transitional coalitions, actors have gathered energy more to block government machinery,

---

[148] Details on the terms strategic groups and conflicting groups are provided later in this study

undermining and trapping them reciprocally. It should, for instance be noticed that within the framework of the 1+4 coalition from the Sun City peace agreements for the DRC until 2006, the transition government was not at all concerned with the governance of the country. Actors (one president and four vice-presidents) were busier setting traps against each other than working for the country. Each of them became active to ensure his/her physical and political survival after the transitional period.[149] In such a climate of mistrust in which sworn enemies were compelled by the magic of power sharing to go hand in hand, the country was neither managed nor ruled. When these elephants continued fighting, ants that the people represent were simply struggling along for survival. The same climate type was noticed in Ivory Coast, in 2007, where Laurent Gbagbo was obliged to share power with Guillaume Soro, following the Ouagadougou peace agreements until the 2010 elections.[150] The same phenomenon took place in the young South-Sudan Republic between President Salva Kiir and for vice president turn rebel leader, Riek Machar.[151] Deadly fights (at least 300 deaths) that resumed in Juba from July 8th to 11th 2016 between President Salva Kiir's armed forces and those of former vice president Riek Machar demonstrated once more that power sharing was a fake political trade-off whose sociopolitical implementation is a real political and diplomatic challenge.

These political and socio-psychological tragedies generally find an outcome in elections that enshrine the end of the transition and sharing of power according to the terms of the peace agreement. At this

---

[149] I had the opportunity to reside in the DRC and associate with politicians from 2004 to 2006 as the Executive Secretary of a German NGO which organized and transported medical materials for the Kitambo hospital in Kinshasa. I have been a visiting lecturer to DRC every year since 2012 in several protestant universities and also as the Executive Secretary of the Network of African Protestant Universities.

[150] Meetings between Ivorian delegations were held from March 3rd to 5th, 2007 and resulted in the signing of a political agreement between President Laurent Gbagbo and the rebel head, Guillaume Soro on March 4th. Hence, the same year on March 29th, Gbagbo appointed Soro Prime Minister, paving the way to a process that led to the 2010 elections, whose outcome is the post-electoral crisis that subsequently followed.

[151] On February 1st, Salva Kiir, the South-Sudanese president and his former vice president, Riek Machar who had become a rebel head signed a document for a future national unity transition government in Addis Ababa.

level, the second indisputable finding that stems from most peace agreements whose conceptual base has been the Power Sharing mechanism between governments and armed rebels or political opponents, has given way to the organization of elections that, in turn, ended in conflictual as well as dangerous form of polarization for sociopolitical stability in the countries in question. The winner takes all and the loser does not only lose everything but is also stripped of all including his/her freedom. Winning actors have found one of the most tragic solutions which is the total negation of the loser who has lost the touch in political and military force balance. The negation of the loser is demonstrated in his/her exclusion and his/her political destruction and possibly his/her physical elimination. This is how, for example, as a substitute to the south-African type of reconciliation, Congolese and Ivoirians have opted for retributive justice which, as the war and the liberal majority democratic model, could not help in transcending and transforming the conflict but postpones it to a future date. Laurent Gbagbo and Jean Pierre Bemba were, fairly or not, delivered to the International Criminal Court by their adversaries and yesterday's allies; Riek Machar went into exile to save his life. In any case, conflicts turning into violence are just postponed till after. [152] Thus, community frustration outcomes are the seeds for future conflicts between biological, ideological and political children and grandchildren of current actors who settle accounts with the negation of the other's humanity and not with mutual forgiveness and reconciliation.

---

[152] Jean Pierre Bemba has been acquitted from the charges of war crimes and crimes against humanity on the June 8, 2018 by the Appeals Chamber of the International Criminal Court. This fact is another indicator of the political instrumentalization of the ICC by the winners and of the failure of Power Sharing as political conflict resolution mechanism in divided societies. Riek Machar and Salva Kiir have signed another peace agreement in July 2018 that is yet to be implemented with the return of Riek Machar in Juba.

<h1 style="text-align:center">CHAPTER 3</h1>

<h2 style="text-align:center">Democratic Rotation in High Office[153]</h2>

In the current wave of democratization processes in most countries in the continent, the question one may raise is whether African countries could positively and proudly not take responsibility for their diverse sociopolitical and ethnic context and focus on a democracy model which does not only take into account this diversity, but which could equally put an end to or at least alleviate conflicts which in most cases, are based on access to supreme power in territorial spaces where their sovereignty reigns. The wish expressed by Bayart in the aftermath of the kick-off of the various democratization processes that: *…African regimes resulting from institutional strain of the fifth French Republic could have had hybridization and re-invention process in a different way…*[154] is still up-to-date. To this re-invention of a *different way*, one would add today, another model of democracy. The success of good governance, of each and everyone's participation and finally, of the development within the perspective of Positive Peace would depend on the re-invention of this specific model for Africa.

Confronted with the Rwanda experience where two decades following the 1994 hideous genocide, the power in place thinks that they can eradicate the evil spirits of genocide by wiping the slate clean on ethnic references between Tutsi, Hutu and Twa in official documents, we see the threat that this might be a headlong rush through which sons and daughters of Rwanda refuse to take into account the living together issue between these three ethnic groups, within the same territorial space, in order to find a sustainable political and ap-

---

[153] In the German version I put it as follow: "Demokratisches Rotationsprinzip" and French one: "Démocratie Rotative". Sometime in this English version the concept has been translated as "Rotative Democracy". But *Democratic Ration in High Office* is the best translation that brings the core idea of the concept out.

[154] Bayart, Jean François: op.cit.p11

propriate solution which enables their sociopolitical acceptance and participation. Having reached the mega-conflict level, we support Achille Mbembe who thinks that the deconstruction of the current construction materials must go through *a full knowledge of the status of our inevitably provincial speeches and necessarily regional concepts – and therefore through a review of any type of abstract universalism...*[155] It is not by discarding references to the Tutsi, Hutu and Twa in speeches and official documents that Tutsi and Hutu will stop being what they have become over the time through a process of intractable identity construction in the great lakes region of Africa. The deconstruction will take place through a double movement of transcendence and transformation in consciousness and not through a pathetic and emotional negation of realities based on sociopolitical hypocrisy of its current product. This is a typical case of negative transcendence according to Galtung. As Melchior Mbonimpa has clearly put it, *There are tribes in Africa. They have to be taken into account or better: they should be relied on. We cannot promote democracy behaving as if the free competition of political "parties" will eclipse tribes' conflict because this conflict is not simply a childhood disease of post-colonial states. In current Africa, a society without tribes is only the fallacy of those fascinated by short-cuts and in a haste to enjoy themselves mistakenly, because the frantic and pathetic back-flow which is making people disregard what is obvious (that the tribe is livelier than ever, for better and for worse) can only lead to disaster...*[156] This is why, for him *In Africa, whoever pretends that the tribal man must die to give birth to the new man, the superior man or simply the citizen, is dwelling on fantasies...*[157] This reality is not specific to Africa. Even, in old western democracies, regional diversity is not, in any case, an obstacle to individual freedom, to democracy, and least a shame to humanity. German national identity and German democracy does not suffer at all from the regional consciousness displayed by Bavarians, the Saxons or the Berliners..., all

---

[155] Mbembe, Achille: Politique de l'inimitié, Editions La Découverte, Paris 2016, P.17

[156] Mbonimpa, Melchor: Ethnicité et Démocratie en Afrique, l'homme tribal contre l'homme citoyen ? L'Hamattan 1994, p. 7

[157] Ibid. p.11

these regional and ethnic identities are visible in highways, in federal and regional institutions and are bursting with historical and cultural wealth, values and human competencies that make the pride of the whole German Nation and constitute German contribution to Universality.

To return to the African case, without being an essentialist, we support cardinal Christian Tumi when he writes: Each of our tribes is the World Creator's will and any cultural value which is in accordance with the World Creator's will is a great wealth for all the humanity …In each tribe, there are men and women capable of working for our common good.[158]Consequently, the ethnic group per se is not an obstacle to democracy in Africa. Disregarding the existence of ethnic groups as it was the case in the various processes on the eve and in the aftermath of independences has only postponed their management difficulties to future generations. Our generation is already testing it acutely. According to Mbonimpa, Democracy in Africa will not spare the effort to think in order to restore the tribal existence without renewing the pyramidal paradigm inherited from the barbaric times.[159]It is, thus, clear. But how do we go about this rehabilitation of the ethnic group within the postcolonial state in Africa without falling into the trap of Power Sharing that clearly comes out in Mbonimpa's words and whose model perpetuates the patronage link between the center and the periphery? How do we carry out this kind of sociopolitical reconciliation between the ethnic group and the Nation-State through democracy while escaping the easy solution of one-size fits all power sharing[160] or better the "ethno-federalism" as proposed elsewhere for Ethiopia?[161] The ethnic group does not disappear with the Democratic Rotation in high office. The presentation of the conceptual framework of this model in the light of Cameroon

---

[158] Wiyghansaï Shaaghan Tumi, Christian in: Les deux Régimes Politiques d' Ahmadou Ahidjo, Macacos, 2006, p.128

[159] Mbonimpa, Melchor: op.cit. pp.11–12

[160] Rothchild, Donald: Durable peace after Civil war: the structuring of ethnic interaction ULPA, Leipzig 2002, pp. 6–8

[161] Assefa, Gidey: Ethnonationale Konflikte, Föderalismus und Demokratie in Äthiopien. Online Veröffentlichung, Frankfurt am Main 2002, p.178.

and Ivory Coast case studies will certainly reopen the debate on democratization in Africa, plural societies, good governance and development.

**Examples of Rotating Presidency and Rotation of the Outer-space**

Before presenting the conceptual framework of the Democratic Rotation, it is important to see if and how similar approaches have been put in place in several forms of political organization. It is clear that the rotating presidency is a management method well used within international organizations. According to this operating mode, the president of the organization is temporarily chosen in accordance with parameters depending on his/her nationality, his/her origin, his/her territory. There is no election. In general, everything has been pre-arranged many years before. Each country (or each community…) knows when it is their turn to be president. This practice allows small countries or militarily, economically and demographically weak countries to also have access to power, to influence decision-making and defend their interests. This operating mode is, certainly, criticized for the unstable nature of its decision-makers and the possible discontinuity of political guidelines, but it reinforces commitment and the sense of belonging of each member state within the organization and prevents frustration. One would say a positive transcendence.

*The UN and the EU[162]*

The rotating power principle is put in place at the presidency level of the security council of the **United Nations Organization**. Each council member state runs the presidency for a month. The rotation order is alphabetical depending on the name of the member states in English language. Another principle which is unwritten but that is

---

[162] It is certainly true that at the level of these positions within International Organizations, the power is undermined by the power ratio between international actors. But the psychological effect of the rotating presidency has alleviated the fears and pride of small and big countries, thus facilitating their membership. It should be noted that it took centuries not only for the Zeitgeist to grow but especially for everyone to be sure of their survival for international organizations such as the UN, the EU … be created. Emanuel Kant and others had long hope to see them before the century of the enlightenment.

also observable in the history of the United Nations' General Secretaries is that starting from 1953 with Birman U Thant, this position started rotating between continents. As a matter of fact, after the Birman Asian **U Thant** (1961–1971) there was the Austrian European **Kurt Waldheim** (1972–1981); the Peruvian Latin-American **Javier Pérez de Cuéllar** (1982–1991); the Egyptian African **Boutros Boutros-Ghali** (1992–1996) ; the Ghanaian African **Kofi Annan** (1997–2006),[163]following by the South-Korean Asian **Ban Ki-Moon** (2007–2016), the position returned to Europe in 2017 to the Portuguese **Antonio Guterres**.

Even though it is not a State strictly speaking, the **European Union** in its structure and operation mode is close to a State. Still, it is the ultimate illustration of this federation of Republican States with the cosmopolitan citizen that Emmanuel Kant introduced way back in 1795 in order to put an end to wars in Europe at that time.[164]In order to promote the integration of all members in terms of acceptance and participation, a system of rotating presidency was established in the European Union Council. In fact, from the treaty of Maastricht (1991/1993) to that of Lisbon (2007/2009) including those of Amsterdam (1997/1999) and Nice (2001/2003), it was provided that the presidency of the European Union Council is rotating. This meant that each member state takes turn for the presidency of the European Union for a period of six months. The aim of this provision was to boost the involvement of leaders and the people of the concerned country to reinforce their sense of belonging to the European Union.[165]In this supranational European organization, the rotation order

---

[163] One of the reasons behind the succession of two Africans is that Boutros Boutros Ghali had been unable to have two terms and it would have been unfair to deprive the African continent of its second term to this effect. The misfortune of the Egyptian will then be a blessing for the African continent with a total of three successive terms at the head of this international organization.

[164] Kant, Immanuel: Kleinere Schriften zur Ethik und Religionsphilosophie, 1870 Bd.I P.150.

[165] Article 203 of the Amsterdam Treaty provides that "each member state takes turn at the presidency for a six months period according an order set by the unanimous Council." The Nice Treaty makes the same provision and a council decision re-states it as follows: "The order of the rotation of member states at the council presidency from January 1st, 2007 is fixed in the appendix"

is alphabetical depending on the name of the country in its own language.

### *The African Union and the Union of the Comoros*

Just like the European Union, the presidency of the **African Union** follows the same rotating principles. The basis of the rotating presidency term of office has moved from six months at the beginning to one year. Each African country takes the presidency of the African Union or of the Commission on a rotation basis.

The **Union of the Comoros** is an African country made up of four islands (Grande-Comore, Moheli, Anjouan and Mayotte) located at the entrance of Mozambique Channel, to the north-east of Madagascar. An overseas territory in 1946, the archipelago of the Comoros gained its independence in 1975 with Moroni as capital city which voted for a definitive integration into France in 1976. The country underwent a long period of political instability with successive coups and dictatorial regimes until 2001, when the rotating presidency was adopted to manage rivalries and other power fights in the islands.[166] According to this principle a native of each island takes turn in the presidency of the Union. The president of the Union is only responsible for the external affairs and the defense of the country. The Islands' presidents autonomously manage the economic and financial sectors, health and justice. The May 22$^{nd}$ 2009 referendum gave way to the adoption of a new constitution which grants more prerogatives to the President of the Union. Islands Presidents become governors with council assemblies. It is clear in this case that with the December 23$^{rd}$ 2001 constitution, the rotating presidency was introduced in the Comoros as a response to political pressure from separatist or secessionist movements. It put an end to cycles of government coups[167] and thus contributed to political stability and democratic change in the Comoros. The only thing that might be reviewed here are primary elections organized in the Island on which the rotating

---

[166] Refer to article 13 of the Constitution of the Union of Comoros of December, 2001.

[167] It should be noted that there was an attempt of power overthrow from the 19–20, April 2013 but which resulted in a failure.

presidency falls and not within the political parties. This reduces the number of candidates to three only, thus limiting the competition between political parties with their various programs.

## *Rotating Movement of the Cosmos*

The rotating principle per se is of cosmological order. It docks in perfectly with the dynamics of the universe, with its visible and invisible physical phenomena, with its discovered and undiscovered laws. In the universe that is in the outer space of the solar system in which the globe is found, planets rotate on themselves either prograde or regressive wise (rotation) and around the solar system (revolution). Even around the earth, satellites launched by human beings are in a permanent rotating movement around the earth. This means that the universe per se is against static bodies. Everything is in a rotating motion; everything moves in order to create balance and equilibrium. Every static body, therefore, can only upset the balance and disrupt the evolution and the revolution of the cosmos. There is therefore a permanent renewal of position in a well-synchronized overall movement to avoid clashes. Linear movements as those of the comets resulting from the solar rotating movement create accidents when they collide with other celestial bodies and planets.

Transposed to human societies with the earth planet being an integral part of the solar galaxy, one easily understands why anybody, any organ, any social organization, any structure which does not move, which is not in a permanent renewal dynamics, is doomed to suffocate and die. One can also therefore understand why it is by the simple strength of the evolving nature of the spirit of time (Zeitgeist) and after several centuries that strong empires, kingdoms and absolute monarchies that the humanity has witnessed from the Pharaonic Egypt to the Moroccan Kingdom as well as Ancient Greece, the big Roman Empire, Mesopotamia, Great Britain and other principalities whose governance principle is linear and logically static. They have been unable to withstand the revolutionary massive up-rising of crowds that were requesting nothing more than their freedom and the respect for their dignity. For the most majority, all these forms of social organization, which in their operating and functioning system were against the cosmos renewing and dynamic order, have one after the other, either been fully dismantled or simply minimized to what are known today as a few honorary and notability titles constitutionally well-framed. A few absolute monarchies can still withstand on earth but only thanks to the blind submission of their people to manipulative religious ideologies. They form a very weak percentage of the world population and take up a tiny fraction of the world space.[168] One may wonder for how long? Maybe still for a long time, but certainly not eternally.

Anything that is static, that does not change, that is against change is against the rotating and dynamic nature of the cosmos, is thus doomed to a tragic end; as it would eternally not withstand the natural forces generated by the power of the rotating strength of the cosmos which, in turn, impacts human societies. Clashes and collisions of the cosmos express themselves in terms of popular revolutions on the globe, revolutions that can be avoided through a rational and intelligent organization of the access to power and its management in a perpetual dynamism.

## Conceptual Bases of the Democratic Rotation in High Office

Inspired by the advantages of the rotating presidency and executive secretary of international organization institutions, and by the importance of the rotating dynamics of planets and heavenly bodies for the solar system order and balance, the Democratic Rotation in the position of the head of state stands as a response to the lack of political and economic development that plagues countries with socio-cultural diversity, that is politically speaking, not yet transcended. However, two variables must be determined and identified for the implementation of the Rotation in a given country: **the Strategic**

---

[168] Here, we are talking of absolute monarchies which include Qatar, Brunei, UAE, Oman and the Vatican. They cover only 2.559,451 Km2 with a total of 26,535,000 inhabitants. For these statistics, refer to https://fr.sputniknews.com/infographies/20130403197984290/ checked on February, 11th, 2017 at 9.38pm.

**Group and the Conflicting Groups (SG/CG).**[169] Depending on the context, a group may have several indicators as constituting parameters of the solidarity between members: ethnic, racial, religious belonging etc. Both types of groups, indeed, have the same characteristics but aspire to contradicting political objectives depending on their position in political spectrum in place. For a group of population to be considered, it must have:

1. A common identity link and a strong solidarity mechanism between members;

2. A constructed or in-born cultural and traditional legitimation;

3. An ideological coherence at the cultural and political level and a geographical emotional reference;

4. A community historical legacy;

5. An elite that claims its sense of belonging to the group and has at least one charismatic leader;

6. A popular mobilization potential which can be a threat to everyone's stability.

Whether it is the Strategic group or the Conflicting group, the power and threat potential that the respective elite have, result from two factors namely:

1. The legitimation of a cultural, religious or historical tradition;

2. The mobilization potential based on subjective or objective community link.

Elements of ideological coherence, of the internal unity or of sacred union allow the analysis of internal contradictions within the same group in order to understand the opportunistic positioning of the con-

---

[169] The SGCG is a reproduction of a conceptual framework designed by a group of German political scientists who with Prof. Dr. Rainer Tetzlaff of Hamburg University worked on democratization difficulties in developing countries in Asia, Latin America and Africa in the 1990s. Refer to Schubert, Gunter & al.: Demokratisierung und politischer Wandel. Hamburg 1994.

flicting groups' elite in relation to the strategic group and to explain the policy of subsidized patronage that the strategic group uses to weaken the coherence of conflicting groups.

## Strategic Group

According to the SG/CG concept, a group is said to be strategic when its members get control of the core of the administrative and institutional powers of the State. It has a hand on the state security apparatus and the institutional mechanism of resource distribution at all levels. It has the monopoly of legal power of the state and controls all sources of public income. It is the group from which comes the Head of State, the President of the Republic and which is thus at the *center of power*. Against the backdrop of political patronage, this group mobilizes the advantages of its strategic position to monopolize the political power as long as possible. At the political level, power balance is in favor of the members of the Strategic Group and this is how their elite manipulate the population with xenophobic and ethnocentric speeches and vote buying, in order to ensure their unwavering support and vote during elections. Even if this mass lives in abject poverty, it supports its elite on a simple objective or subjective solidarity identity link. It is the electoral stronghold of the political party of the Head of State. This group strategically brings as allies a few moderate elites of the conflicting groups into the power circle through political patronage, assigning to them a few unimportant resources with regard to the political power and the management of public affairs.

## Conflicting Groups

Contrary to the strategic group, Conflicting Groups are at the *periphery of power,* and have a potential threat of political destabilization. They are held off on the state apparatus and are, thus, nursing a feeling of political frustration. The hardliners among the elite of these groups refuse political alienation to the Strategic Group and also mobilize their respective masses to challenge the existing power balance. Conflicting Groups contest the Strategic Group's powerful position and power monopolization tendencies. In a democracy or democratization context, they serve as political bases for the opposition political parties or a backseat of an armed rebellion in the case of a militarized meso-conflict. These groups aim at:

1.  Reversing the political power balance in order to control the state apparatus;

2.  Perpetuating their identity and historical legacy from one generation to another;

3.  Defending themselves against assimilative tendencies and cultural homogenization of the hegemonic group.

In short, a link of political patronage, if not, of *enmity*, *"un lien d'inimitié"*, is building up between the Strategic Group at the center of power and the Conflicting Groups at the periphery. The Strategic Group is *inside* and the Conflicting groups are *outside* of political power.[170] If the political patronage or the relationship of sinecures does not work with regard to the dominant and the dominated, the crushing of the other is just a matter of circumstance. Both groups hate one another, abuse one another, slap themselves with clichés, do not tolerate one another and coexist in a kind of cold psychosocial war until one day, a spark is triggered and violence and enmity take over dialogue and reason.

### *Electoral System with Rotating Candidacy*

After identifying the Strategic Group and the Conflicting Groups, the electoral system must be designed in such a way that all important groups have the possibility of ascending to the highest office of the Head of State in a given country through democratic elections, in which every citizen of the State can cast a vote.

If groups prove to be emotionally attached to specific geographical references, as it is the case in several countries on the continent, rotation at the High Office, that is, the Presidency of the Republic should take place on the basis of two electoral terms per **Electoral Region** as in Cameroon and Ivory Coast. Conversely, if the historical process

---

[170]  For the concepts, refer to Mbembe, Achille: op.cit (2016) p.58

of population mixture and spatial intermingling has reached a certain level of indisputable geographic integration and the identity element of the group is, thus, deterritorialized, the rotation cycle at the head of the state will follow, not in terms of order between the regions but the order of rotation according to dividing lines between floating identities. That is identities that meet exclusion and inclusion criteria, having indeed taken on space, but still withstand the time of political sensibilities. It could be race as in the case with South-Africa or the USA, or even deterritorialized ethnic elements like between the Hutus and Tutsis in the Great Lakes Region of Africa.

### *Operating Mode*

The Democratic Rotation in High Office needs the following steps for the choice of candidate, the electoral campaign and elections per se:

1. Political parties, in accordance with internal standards of candidate nomination for presidential elections, will choose their candidate from the group or region that has the rotation term. All candidates are from the same group or region, but from different political gatherings with different political programs or plate forms;

2. Political parties will campaign nationwide for their respective candidate. It is all the people that make the state in question that is going to vote for the President of the Republic and will thus ensure not only his/her popular legitimacy but also the democratic aspect of rotation;

3. After two terms of (7 years x 2) or (5 years x 2) in a given group or region, the rotation principle will allow the next group or region to have access to the High Office, so on and so forth;

4. Following two to four rotation terms at the position of the Head of the State, a new generation of citizens, used to peaceful political alternations because of the Democratic Rotation in the position of the President, will emerge being well pre-

pared for liberal democracy if they believe it is necessary at all.

Democratic Rotation in High Office will, thus, bring about a new political fact: elite must mobilize members of its group to vote for the candidate of its political party not in a unique sense as over decades, but in a spirit of change. This is how, exclusive and inclusive identity elements will deteriorate themselves and will be transcended and transformed positively into a new situation in which the acceptance and the participation of everyone become sociopolitical normalcies. Democratic Rotation in High Office, therefore, stands as a solution:

1. Against political exclusion which generates frustrations of conflicting groups at the periphery of power and victims of social stigmatization;

2. Against the sociopolitical fear of the Strategic Group and often demographically in a minority. Being at the center of power, they do not want to lose it for good through the principle of democratic majority, and is craving for the monopolization of power by all means. Rotation alleviates this fear;

3. Against political vote buying and political patronage between elites in the center and those at the periphery;

4. Against anti-democratic short-cuts of Power Sharing;

5. For an integration policy through the acceptance of diversity and the possibility for everyone to participate, thus overcoming diversity;

6. For a peaceful non-violent political climate suitable for political alliances based on programs between political parties and not on selfish motivations of the elite.

**Legal and Sociopolitical Safeguards**

At the national and international levels, legal provisions and some institutional reforms are necessary for the implementation of the rotating principle at the position of the Head of the State.

### *At the National level*

At the national level, the constitution is the first legal instrument to guarantee the rotating principle. The constitution must make provision that the position of the President of the Republic is rotating according to a number of terms determined by regions in the case of geographically identifiable social groups, if there is a deterritorialized diversity. The electoral code and the body that manages the election will hook on to this constitutional provision to bring more details for practice.

### *Neutral Army and Public Administration*

The national army and public administration are two republican institutions that must be reformed. Provided that the army and public administration in all its sectors are financed by the taxes of all citizens of a country, these two professional corps must be apolitical. Their political neutrality must be enshrined in the constitution. The army and civil servants must be accorded prerogative not to obey a President who could be finding a way to block the rotation cycle. When these two conditions are legally and practically met, an external body from the administration for the organization of elections is no longer necessary: the transparency of elections is thus guaranteed by the neutrality of public administration and the national army as is the case in old western democracies.

### *At the International Level*

In a transitory phase, the country that takes on the Democratic Rotation in High Office must provisionary delegate some level of its sovereignty to supranational bodies. Its international, bi-and multilateral cooperation for development becomes a rotation protection tool.

*Rotation Protection by the AU and the UN*

At the level of African countries that take on the practice of Democratic Rotation in High Office, a permanent request for intervention must be made to the *Peace and Security Council*[171] of the African Union through its *African Standby Force* tool and through similar tools within sub-regional organizations in the case that a President in power wants to block the rotation cycle in the High Office of his/her country.[172] This provision, made at the beginning of the rotation cycle, would prevent legally questionable actions and interferences with regard to international law as was the case in Gambia, often quoted as a case of law for Rotation protection. The baseline is to formally apply at the supranational bodies, for what Djiby Sow describes as *the intervention right to restore constitutional legitimacy and order in a State following a coup or an electoral holdup...*[173] Such a provision of standing mandate for the protection of the Democratic Rotation in High Office can be broadened at the United Nations Security Council which is ultimately the only guarantor of international peace and security. It is a kind of *democratic interference right*. It would be a giant step in Africa which has to get out of the birthplace of humanity and assert itself as an independent and important actor in the process of the worldwide sustainable development.

*Respect for Rotation as ODA Conditionality*

After a burnout of development paradigms was enshrined by the adoption of the MDGs in 2000, and subsequently by the SDGs in

---

[171] In conformity with article 5 (2) of the Constitutive Act of the African Union, the Peace and Security Council is *a permanent body for conflict prevention, management and settlement.*

[172] Similar to the African Union intervention in Comoros in 2008 ("Freedom and reconciliation operation" to chase Colonel Mohamed Bacar out of Anjouan or the intervention of the West-African sub-regional organization (ECOWAS) in January 2017 ("re-establishing democracy operation") to bring Yahya Jammeh to concessions in the post-electoral crisis, thus, saving peace and democracy in the Gambia.

[173] Sow, Djiby: Crise gambienne: rétrospective juridique sur l'intervention militaire de la CEDEAO in: http://www.wathi.org/laboratoire/tribune/crise-gambienne-retrospective-juridique-lintervention-militaire-de-cedeao/ consulted on 13/02/2016 à 11H10

2015, the respect of Democratic Rotation in High Office becomes a new conditionality of international cooperation for development through its ODA tool across all sectors and with all bilateral and multilateral actors. The ODA suspension and economic sanctions become protector levers of Democratic Rotation in the position of the Head of State.

The bottom line is that Democratic Rotation will certainly not resolve all the problems of a diverse state, but it would help to address the frustrations caused by the feelings of exclusion and marginalization, any bitterness and any fear of CG/SG in a given State. Each citizen, regardless of his/her membership or origin, can hope, some day, to run his/her country through the act of law that in most constitutions ensures it, but through the act of *Realpolitik* where political negative clichés and stigmatization make people say that it would be inacceptable that a native of such and such groups gets access to power. The basic advantage of the Democratic Rotation is in everyone's feeling of mutual acceptance, in the possibility to participate in power, thereby providing sources of political stability that is of peace and subsequently, a prerequisite for development. It proves to be, for all intents and purposes, an element of socio-political equity for the SG/CG, for the national community rather than for individuals.

### Socio-political Safeguards

Whether at the national or international level, the key to a political success of the Democratic Rotation is *forgiveness and reconciliation between African generations.* The current generation, the post-independence generation and especially the 1970s – 1980s generation must acknowledge what our parents have made as sacrifice in the resistance against historical attacks. We should also forgive them for the past and current shortcomings in the negotiation and management of relationships with others in order to reconcile with our past and face it up in an intelligent manner. *Acknowledgment* helps get rid of the fear of self-flagellation. Forgiveness would be the lever on which to redefine together new bases on which to build social cohesion. *Forgiveness* provides enough largeness of mind to be able to ensure a peaceful retirement on the African soil to our parents, who bore the heavy responsibility for managing our countries under the historical conditions that we know. Compelling them to a leap into the unknown of the exile is only counter-productive for us. Witch hunt will not move us ahead but will most likely increase our chances of going deeper into a misplaced inter and intra generational cycle of hatred.

Still at the socio-political level, *policies of regional balance or affirmative action and power sharing* must be kept with a certain level of meritocracy in the sharing of other political, administrative and economic resources.

Finally, a *blanket amnesty for corruption* would be necessary before the provision of new governance and management regulations with related sanctions applicable to all. Witch hunt simply postpones hatred, bitterness and violence. A child born in a family that he/she did not choose and who suffers from humiliation caused by detention of his/her parents, perpetrators of corruption, is a potential warmonger. And it is human. The general blanket amnesty for corruption will prevent us from creating future rebel leaders. The real keystone to social and political *reconciliation* is the practice of non-violent conflict transformation. With non-violence one can kill violence and not the violent; can kill corruption by educating the corrupter and not by crushing him. It is one of the conditions for defining bases for a new departure for a future social cohesion without impunity.

Democratic Rotation in High Office could be criticized for wanting to perpetuate what Mbembe has called *juxtaposition of peculiarities,* and it would, as such, be an obstacle to the universality. This appears at first sight, because Democratic Rotation in High Office actually allows peculiarities at the local level to mutually accept each other and to express in political act their sense of *co-belonging and sharing*[174] to and in a common national space. At the local level, it is a response to the process of *democracy exit*[175] that Mbembe has observed at the global level in the frenetic struggle against globalized

---

[174] Mbembe, Achille: op.cit p.57

[175] Ibid. pp17–59

terrors. The mismatch of liberal democracy to divided societies has led political entrepreneurs to develop bypasses for the rules of political games. Here too, the rule of law *can only be protected by the law. It cannot be through lawlessness*[176]. At the local level, Democratic Rotation will give way to a non-simplistic integration because it is not forced or resulting from political grandstanding, but a conscious integration wanted by peculiarities that accept each other, respect each other, tolerate each other and acknowledge equal opportunities of participation and same talents of management of the state at the highest level. Democratic Rotation thus makes of « *l'en-commun* » *(the togetherness)*[177] a real possibility at the level of States. It provides ethnic groups whether imagined or not with the idea of a single state territory, common to all and which makes everyone at the same time and at all levels les « *ayants droit, toutes espèces confondues*» *(the right holders of any kinds)*[178]. The enmity link is, thus, transcended and transformed into a new situation acceptable to all groups. No group, any longer feels threatened to disappear or no longer has a deep sense of frustration caused by the domination from another group. The full development of this *local togetherness* is the precondition to the advent of a *global togetherness* in which our single world is a property in equal shares for all cosmopolitan citizens.

---

[176] Ibid. p.49

[177] The "l'en-commun" concept of Mbembe should be understood as a new manner of expressing universality and not with regard to uniformity, but rather as an expression of differences that accept one another, tolerate each other valorize and exchange as equals in Senghor's meeting-place for giving and receiving, a space under everlasting construction, deconstruction and reconstruction.

[178] Ibid. P.59

# CHAPTER 4

## Projecting Democratic Rotation into practical cases

### Deterritorialized Identities (Rwanda, Burundi, USA, SA)

Here, the inclusion or exclusion element is not linked to any geographical origin. There has been a spatial missing of individuals to the extent that the identity criterion is floating or deterritorialized. It is the case in the United States of America, South-Africa or Rwanda, where one would not say that White, Black or Hispanic Americans are identifiable by a specific territorial anchoring. The same applies to south-Africans, where blacks and whites share the same territories despite the Bantustans of the Apartheid era.

**In Rwanda** for example, it is difficult to identify regions of origins of Tutsi and Hutu. Both ethnic groups have shared and are still sharing the same geographical space. Being the outcomes of socio-political and professional construction, we are hoping that with the new political situation, which consists in eradicating references to the ethnic group of Rwandese citizens, future generations will succeed in transcending this suicidal cleavage between the Hutu and the Tutsi in the three countries of the Great Lakes Region namely; Rwanda, Burundi and Uganda. In anticipation of the transcendence and transformation of identities entrenched in these three countries, starting from the option taken by the current power in Kigali, the introduction of Democratic Rotation in High Office will consequently provide each product of the identity construction that are made up of the current ethnic groups, with a possibility of taking turns in the seat of the President of the Republic. The rotation cycle would be based on ethnic groups and not on regions. Democratic Rotation would thus imply that in turns, either Tutsi or Hutu dominated political parties at some point have to choose their presidential election candidate from the Hutu group and later from the Tutsi group. The Hutu would then campaign for a Tutsi and later on the Tutsi would mobilize their people for a Hutu candidate. The Rwanda Patriotic Front (RPF) of President Kagame (Tutsi) would be compelled to nominate a Hutu candidate for presidential elections. It would be a true socio-political trigger in this country that has become a typical model of growth and development within 20 years.[179]

**In Burundi,** the NCDD-DDF[180] of President Pierre Nkurunziza (Hutu) will have to choose a Tutsi candidate for presidential elections. And finally in Uganda, the National Resistance Movement (NDR) of President Yoweri Museveni (Tutsi) will be compelled by the Rotation law to choose a Hutu candidate for the next presidential elections, thus giving away the power that he has had since 1986 to a Hutu and this is with the strong hope and assurance that a Tutsi will come back to it soon. It is from this mutual acceptance that a real transcendence and transformation of ethnicity between the Hutu and the Tutsi will result not from a top-down diktat, but from the bottom of the hearts and souls of the people of Burundi, Rwanda and Uganda, thus, deeply reconciled between themselves and with themselves.

**In the United States of America,** the history of this country has required that former masters and slaves of plantations share the same regions with certainly different public space. This has resulted in a kind of deterritorialized identity even if there are federate states with white or black predominance. Democratic Rotation in High Office would want that the Republican and the Democratic Parties, for example, take compulsory rotation terms to present to their respective voters only two black candidates and then two white candidates. This will, thus provide Black and White Americans with the opportunity to have regular change between Black and White in the White House without it being a niche as it was the case for President Barack Obama in 2007. White segregationists and black radicals will take turns to swallow this bitter pill and either vote for a Black or a White

---

[179] In my teaching-adventure life, since 2008, I have been quite a regular visitor to the great lakes region and the country of one thousands hills is one of the compulsory stops in my journey. Any honest observer would have a hard time to deny the infrastructural transformation that the country is undergoing every year.

[180] NCDD-DDF: National Council for the Defense of Democracy/ Democracy Defense Forces is the political party currently in power in Bujumbura.

or else do not vote at all. There is no guarantee that this will remove racism from the United States, but at least frustration from some Americans and the arrogance of others caused by the complex of racial inferiority, on the one hand and superiority on the other, would give way to a feeling of acceptance and participation in the hearts and souls of a large majority of American people.

**In South-Africa**, the introduction of the Democratic Rotation between Blacks and Whites will compel the great historical party with the black majority, the African National Congress (ANC) to nominate a White as a candidate for presidential elections when it is the term for the Whites; and the opposition party with a white minority, Democratic Alliance (DA) will nominate a Black candidate for presidential elections when it is the term for Blacks. In the current constellation of Westminster liberal democracy model, it is almost impossible that a White South-African be elected President of the Republic of South-Africa in a near future. Democratic Rotation in the position of the President of the Republic will not only turn this faraway possibility into a near one but will also turn it into a political normalcy in a South-African society which is still healing the wounds of half a century of the human stupidity that Apartheid was, erected in the heart of the 20<sup>th</sup> century and right under the Universal Declaration of Human Rights *both as government ideology and technology* in Mbembe's words.[181] Democratic Rotation would therefore reflect Ubuntu itself and the materialization of the rainbow nation in Realpolitik in South-Africa.

## Geographically Identifiable Identities

Here, there is certainly a geographical dispersal of populations but the general tendency is that each person migrates with an identity whose breeding ground remain the land or origin: an identity that is even magically transmitted to off springs born out of the land of origin and who, for the majority, have never set foot there. Identity by heritage follows them like their shadow. Groups still refer very strongly to their homeland regardless of their place of residence and

---

[181] Mbembé, Achille:op. cit. (2013) p.62

work in the national territory and even abroad. Here, as elsewhere, people come together and organize each other on the basis of community parenthood, of a blood link whose single source of beverage is found in the region of origin. Identity is both ethnic and regional. We will use two specific cases to illustrate this: Ivory Coast and Cameroon.

## Ivory Coast[182]

### *Strategic and Conflicting Groups*

The current geographical space of Ivory Coast has witnessed great migratory moments that led to its settlement,[183] whose formation along the way has resulted in four large ethnic groups which, today, schematically form four ethno-regional electoral strongholds. The country, as a matter of fact, became a French colony on March10, 1893 and Ivoirians were gathered into four main ethnic groups to facilitate colonial administration. This is how the Akan, Krou, Mande, and Gour (Volta Group)[184] ethnic groups progressively prevailed on the Ivoirian political spectrum with exclusive ethno-regional identities. People that form the other ethnic groups, Krou, Mande and Gour successively located in the South-East and the North-East of Ivory Coast were forced to migrate towards the East to contribute to the presence of this region and the development of the Akan ethnic group. For the development of large forest located in the East of the country, people of this region's land were expropriated by

---

[182] Tagou, Célestin: Gestion des Conflits en Afrique: Regards croisés de jeunes chercheurs de l'UPAc ; Revue Africaine de Paix, Communication et Développement, N°001-Nov2011, PUPA 2011, Yaoundé.

[183] Rougerie, Gabriel: *La Côte D'Ivoire,* Que sais-je? PUF, Paris, 1964, p.54.

[184] This classification shows that the *Mande* linguistic group is made up of groups that live in the North-West of the country: *Bambara, Dioula, Foula, Dan...* The *Kru* linguistic group is made up of people settled in the West of the country: *Kru, Bété... the Gur or Volta* linguistic group is made up of people located in the North-East of the country: *Senoufo, Koulango, Lobi...* The *Kwa* linguistic group is made up of people located in the East of the country: *Akan, Agni, Baoulé, Abron, Ebrié...*in: Bouquet, Christian in: op. cit.

European farmers, with the assistance of Baoule farmers of the Akan ethnic group.

On August 7th, 1960 Ivory Coast became independent with Félix Houphouët-Boigny as President of the Republic. With him, the Akan ethnic group got access to central power, and was in fact no longer identified as the ethnic group at the colonial center. Either as the ethnic group at the central power or the strategic group, the Akan ethnic group had to compete in the conservation of the power acquired from the colonial authority with the ethnic groups at the periphery, thereby becoming Conflicting Groups: Mande, Gour (Volta groups) and Krou. All these ethnic groups have developed a strong community identity based on their home region. This sense of belonging to an ethnic group from one's home is an important key for reading actors' behaviors in the political landscape in Ivory Coast since independence.

This map provides an idea on the territorial division of the four large ethnic groups of the people of the Ivory Coast State.

A glimpse at the political elite that has existed in Ivory Coast since independence demonstrates a conflict built around geographic boundaries between the four ethno-regional groups above. We therefore have:

**Félix Houphouët-Boigny:** from Baoule, he became the President of the Ivorian Republic in 1960, thereby making the Akan ethnic group the Strategic Group. Head of the Ivorian state for 33 years, Houphouët-Boigny ruled the country perpetuating the exclusion/inclusion policy and political patronage of the periphery groups' elite. This political patronage allowed the Baoule elite to share income from cocoa and coffee, main economic resources of Ivory Coast, with a few members of the Mande and Gour's elite that they have assimilated. When he passed away in 1993, Houphouët-Boigny was replaced by his constitutional successor, the president of the National Assembly, Henry Konan Bédié as provided by Article 11 of the Constitution of that time.[185]

**Henry Konan Bédié:** equally from Baoule, got access to power after the *old man* (le vieux) and thus maintained the prevalence of Akan ethnic group as the center of authority until 1999, when he was overthrown. In view of keeping the power in the hands of the Akan ethnic group, he adopted an electoral code based on exclusive ethnocentrism during his term of office at the Presidency of the Republic. He was equally the author of an exclusive ethnocentric political speech which spread the political concept of *"Ivoirité"* (Ivority),[186]previously designed by intellectuals from the University Research Unit and Dissemination of Political Ideas and Actions of President Henry Konan Bédié (URUDPIAPHKB).[187] These ethnocentric speeches were

---

[185] Reference: Law n° 94 – 438 of August 16th 1994, revising Law n° 60-356 of November 3rd 1960 on the constitution of Ivory Coast.

[186] The ivority concept was designed by the Baoule elite for the construction of "us", referring to the ethnic group at the central power, and to also refer to pure bred Ivorians against "them", rivaling ethnic groups the majority of which are the people from the North born between 1933–1947. Reference: Bouquet, Christian in: op. cit. p.45

[187] Kipre, Pierre: « Les discours politiques de décembre 1999 à l'élection présidentielle d'octobre 2000: thèmes, enjeux et confrontations » in Le Pape, Marc & Vidal, Claudine (eds): op. cit pp.92–96.

developed by Konan Bédié to exclude his then rival and today's ally, Alassane Dramane Ouattara, from running the competition into the high office.

**Alassane Dramane Ouattara (ADO)**: he is among the people born between 1933 and 1947 in the great Ivory Coast whose nationality continues to feed controversies. Although born in Dimbokro near Yamoussoukro, ADO is the son of a traditional chief of a region located in the current Burkina-Faso. Following his resignation from the government in 1993 and also from the ICDP, he created the Republican Movement (RM) with the blessings of the Mande and Gour elite who also left the ICDP. He henceforth became the spokesperson of the Northern people, whose total population could form a significant electoral weight for the RM. In fact, the 1998 General Census of Population and Habitat (GCPH) indicated that the Mande and Gour ethnic groups successively represented 26.5% and 17.6% of the total population of Ivory Coast, against 42.1% of Akan and 12.7% of Krou.[188] In addition to the religious factor shared by the Mande and Gour ethnic groups, they were equally fighting against the constructed concept of *Ivoirité* developed by the Baoule elite to exclude ADO from running the competition into the Presidency of the Republic. For his fight against the *Ivoirité* and their designers, he gained the support of the elite of another revaling ethnic group, the Krou whose leader was Laurent Gbagbo.

**Laurent Koudou Gbagbo**: native of Mama, a region within the Krou ethnic group, he clandestinely created the Ivorian Popular Front (IPF) in 1982. Forced into exile by the power in place, he returned to the country in the 1990s. Félix Houphouet-Boigny's potential successors were no longer unanimous. On the eve of the 1995 elections, he joined the RM leader to boycott elections and fight against the *Ivoirité* concept that has victimized the Northern people. Together Laurent Gbagbo and ADO created the Republican Front (RF), whose main objective was to fight against the policy and ethnocentric speeches disclosed by the Baoule camp and the ICDP supporters. However, confronted with the political vacuum created on the eve of

---

[188] Bouquet, Christian: op. cit. p.177

the 2000 presidential elections, characterized by the disqualification (by the legal authority) of Henry Konan Bédié and ADO's candidacy for the competition into the High Office, Laurent Gbagbo took advantage of the *Ivoirité* concept to gain the Baoule electorate and increase his chances of being elected at the Presidency. And this happened following elections long described as disastrous, against his ethnic rival Robert Gueï.[189] From this, moment the Ivorian tragedy evolved between these two elite leaders, Gbagbo (Krou ethnic group) and ADO (Volta group), until the fatal demise of the former in 2011. When ADO became President of the Republic, he sent Gbagbo to the International Court of Justice at the Hague. Fairly or not, that is not the question.

**Robert Gueï:** Native of the Krou ethnic group, for a long time he was the Army Chief of staff under Houphouet-Boigny's regime, before being forced into retirement by the Head of Ivorian second republic. The retirement was for a very short period as, he became the head of the military coup in 1999, putting an end to Henry Konan Bédié's regime, largely politically dominated by the Akan ethnic group. This overthrow of the government gave a new ethno-spatial direction to the Ivorian power characterized by the establishment of the Krou ethnic group to the central authority. Unexpectedly, Robert Gueï became candidate for the 2000 presidential elections. Defeated by Laurent Gbagbo and under pressure from the streets, Gueï left power for exile in Benin, before being murdered in 2002 following another military coup, which, this time, failed.[190]

**Guillaume Kigbari Soro:** native of the North, it is within the Ivory Coast Pupils and Students' Association (ICPSA) that he started as a protestor in favor of Robert Gueï's regime. Deprived of the presidency of this association, he joined the RM, then the *Forces Nouvelles* (New Forces: NF), where he had the position of Executive Secretary. In this position, he was identified as the spokesperson of the NF during the mediation that resulted in his appointment, alternately, as

---

[189] Bouquet, Christian: op. cit. p.268

[190] Nguessan, Kouamé: « Le coup d'Etat de Décembre 1999: espoirs et désenchantements ». In Le Pape, Marc & Vidal, Claudine (eds): op. cit. pp.57–69

Minister of Reconciliation and Prime Minister under Laurent Gbagbo's regime. He will subsequently joined ADO's political group in the 2010 elections, and thus, contribute to the downfall of Laurent Gbagbo's regime. Since then, he has been the Speaker of Ivory Coast National Assembly.

Besides the main actors who contributed in one way or another to the development and expansion of inter-ethnic violence in Ivory Coast, there are militia and groups of supporters which have promoted the propensity of ethnocentric ideology in towns and villages. Among militia that represented Mande, Gour and the Extremist Krou rivaling ethnic groups that were claiming the abolition of the *Ivoirité* concept and the rejection of the elections results[191], reference must be made to the Ivory Coast Patriotic Movement (ICPM), the Movement for Justice and Peace (MJP) and the Great West Ivorian Popular Movement (GWIPM).[192] To preserve their claims, these groups merged and gave birth to *Forces Nouvelles* (New Forces: NF) as main actors of the 2002 attempted coup d'état. Against the New Forces were pro-government militia made up of the youth of the ethnic group Krou for the majority and labelled Patriotic Galaxy. Their main goal was *to violently punish opposition demonstrations, to muzzle the press, and to stifle anti-government divisions, in order to instigate a violent anti-foreign sentiment and to attack villages under rebel control in cocoa and coffee producing western regions.[193]* This militia was made of several groups including: Youth Alliance for the National Surge (YANS), Union for the Total Liberation of Ivory Coast (UTLIC), Liberation Forces of the Great West (LFGW), Movement for the Liberation of the West of Ivory Coast (MLWIC), Wê Patriotic Alliance (Wê-PA) and the Patriots' Union for the Great West Resistance (PUGWR).[194]This militia was run by young emblematic

---

[191] Gramizzi, Claudio: « La crise ivoirienne de la tentative de coup d'état au gouvernement de réconciliation nationale »: Rapport du Groupe de recherche et d'information sur la paix et la sécurité (GRIP) Bruxelles, 2003, p.20

[192] Bercovitch, Jacob & al: op. cit. p.114

[193] Rapport de Human Rights Watch: «La meilleure école: La violence estudiantine, l'impunité et la crise en Côte d'Ivoire », Human Rights Watch New York, 2005, p.37

[194] Ibid: pp.14–16

leaders bearing ethno-names established for this purpose: Charles Blé Goudé presented himself as the *General of the youth*, Eugène Djué as the Marshal, and Richard Dakoury as *Sorbonnard*.[195]

From the analysis, it is clear that after more than ten years of inter-ethnic violence perpetrated by various main and secondary actors, the Ivorian conflict has been quite difficult to resolve. Despite multiple negotiation and mediation processes, which finally led to the Ouagadougou political agreement of March 4th 2007, this conflict has had many twists and turns. With this agreement, Power Sharing (between the main stakeholders) has been the way out of the crisis into Negative Peace, whose transformation into Positive Peace had to go through the 2010 elections. Unfortunately, these elections instead gave way to a new post-electoral crisis between 2010 and 2011. The crisis was caused by Gbagbo's refusal to give up power to his challenger, ADO declared winner. According to Gbagbo's political team, the 2010 elections were tainted by a lot of irregularities and fraud, especially in the native region of ADO and Soro, his political ally. According to them, because of these irregularities and fraud, results published by the international community were unacceptable. Following 5 months of a post-electoral deadly conflict, Gbagbo's regime collapsed, he was arrested and ADO was proclaimed Head of State; thus becoming the 5th president of Ivory Coast.

The second observation is that the departure of the *old man* and the advent of democracy plunged Ivory Coast into a cycle of political conflict and violence fed with ethno-regional divisions. All the political changes since 1993 have been violent. The power in turn went from the Akan ethnic group (Houphouët-Boigny, Henri Konan Bédié) to the Gour or Volta ethnic group (Alassane Ouattara) including the Krou ethnic group (Guéi et Gbagbo) not in peace, but with guns and in violence, leaving each time on the floor a defeated, a looser, who loses all and a winner who takes everything. This is not typical of Africa. The defeated shares the feeling of humiliation with his/her ethnic group, which later nurtures the ambition of a future revenge. This clearly demonstrates the failure of the current democ-

---

[195] Bouquet, Christian: op. cit. pp.142–143

racy model in Ivory Coast and that of Power Sharing on whose basis the peace agreements were designed. Hence, there is a need for a change.

### *Rotating Cycle in Ivory Coast*

After 25 years of democratization and Power Sharing, the Jacobin model of liberal democracy and the Power Sharing mechanism have shown their limitations, both as means of conflict resolution and tools of post conflict political management in a divided society such as Ivory Coast. Introducing a Democratic Rotation in the position of the President of the Republic would have created conducive conditions not only for peaceful transition, but also for a consolidation of social cohesion and tolerance that Ivoirians had experimented for 33 years of the *old man's* reign. The High Office, as it is the case, should have gone from the Akan ethnic group since 1990 to the Krou ethnic group and today would be with the Gour ethnic group in three rotation rounds with a 5 years term times 2 per region. This model would also have been a good philosophical basis for the 2007 Ouagadougou Political Agreement and sons and daughters of Ivory Coast would not be dealing today with justice for the winners against the frustrated and humiliated defeated. Notwithstanding, the guarantee for a transcendence and transformation of ethnicity in Ivory coast still has a chance if the current policy chooses to introduce the Democratic Rotation in High Office from 2020, with a five year term mandate renewable once per region between the Gour, Mande, Krou and Akan ethnic groups. The Rotation would be as follows:

**1<sup>st</sup> round: 2020–2030, the President** is Mande (given that the Akan ruled from 1960–1998; the Krou from 1999–2010 and the Gour from 2010–2020)[196]

---

[196] Alasane Ouattara has recently announced his intention to stand for a third term in the 2020 presidential elections in Ivory Caost on the base of the new constitution in spite of the fact that he promised to step down in 2020. The introduction of Democratic Rotation in the Ouagadougou Peace Agreement would have not permitted such a situation which was alike to bring a new cycle of political crisis and ethno regional conflicts in Ivory Coast. But after he has been critized, he stepped from this position in July and announced the passing over power to a new generation of politicians in 2020. Just wait and

**2nd round: 2030–2040: the President is Akan**

**3rd round: 2040–2050: the President is Krou**

**4th round: 2050–2060: the President is Gour** or from the Volta group

In this system, all political parties of Ivory Coast will nominate a native of the ethnic group Mande as their candidate for the 2020 presidential elections, in 2030 a native of the Akan ethnic group, in 2040 a native of the Krou ethnic group and in 2050 a native of the Gour ethnic group. Then all party comrades of all ethnic groups will go on campaign on the Ivorian national territory to request the suffrage of the majority of the Ivorian people for their various nominated candidates. The fact that a Gour native will go to Korhogo and campaign for a native of Krou or Akan or a native of Mande again and vice versa, will create a new peaceful political climate and will rekindle and consolidate the sense of tolerance, acceptance of the other and political participation between Ivorian ethnic groups. Hence, after one or two rotations, a new generation of Ivoirians used to peaceful political changes, will decide to continue with the Democratic Rotation in High Office or to return to the liberal model, with political change as socio-political normalcy.

## Cameroon

### *Ethnographic Landscape*

In the historical, sociopolitical and anthropological literature on Cameroon, 200 to 250 ethnic groups are counted and should constitute the people of the Cameroon State.[197] This surface diversity is the

---

see if he will be fair enough and will not try to manipulate the political outcome in the next years in Côte d'Ivoire and create more ethno-regional conflicts. Despite the fact that, Ouattara is now releasing oppositions leaders (in his speech on 6th August 2010), like Simone Gbagbo, jailed after the 2010 electoral crisis, the introduction of Democratic Rotation, in the Head of State Office, remains the ultimate political solution to transcend and transform ethno-regional conflicts in Ivory Coast.

[197] Mveng, Engelbert: Histoire du Cameroun. Paris 1963. The prelate has established the genealogical tree of the Cameroon ethnic group, with 200 groups; Mbuyinga, Elanga also reported 200 ethnic groups in: Tribalisme et Problème National en Afrique Noire: Le

result of several factors amenable to the settlement history and the geophysical features of Cameroon. Besides the groups of native people that the country has known; the pygmies in the South and the Sao of the far North around Lake Chad, all the other groups that make up today's people of Cameroon come from successive migratory waves. The geographical landscape and the land diversity equally impact behaviors, practices and customs of the various peoples that have progressively settled in the North, the South, the East and the West of Cameroon. Throughout this migration, a social settlement process took place resulting in different groups of population with cultures and languages different from one another. Added to this was the geographical diversity: from the dense tropical forest of the Great South to the almost desert zone of the Great North, one goes through large savannahs, steppes, mountain ranges and plains. This has led Bahoken and Atangana to conclude that: *In Cameroon there are different human types corresponding to the landscape, certain elements of which have contributed to the settlement of peoples in their natural site. They have moulded the spirit of these people and endowed them with particular character traits.*[198] While Walter observes that two main meta-groups have resulted from it, namely: the Sudanese people of the North and the Bantu people of the South.[199] These two diversity factors will therefore impact not only behaviours, practices and customs of the various people that have progressively settled in the North, in the South, in the East or in the West of Cameroon, but also the broad policy guidelines of the country before or after independence. It is in this light that, T Le Vine should be understood when he states: *"Cameroonian political development, then, can be*

---

cas du Kamerun, Ed.L'Harmattan, Paris 1989, p.78; Mono Ndjana, Hubert in: Hubert: L'idée sociale chez Paul Biya, Yaoundé, 1985, p.59. The philosopher has counted 250 groups.

[198] Bahoken, J.C. & Atangana, Engelbert: Cultural policy in the united republic of Cameron. The Unesco Press. Paris 1976, p.9

[199] Nuhn, Walter: Kamerun unter dem Kaiseradler, Neue überarbeitete Auflage, Juni 2000, pp.21–24

*understood only in the light of the interaction between the complex physical and human facts of Cameroon's experience.* "[200]

To better understand the various people between the two large Sudanese and Bantu groups, Mveng, Obenga and Varnier's research activities remain authoritative and are unanimous except on the case of the Bamileke population with two opposite schools of thought: the Tikar and the Bantu-Grassfields.[201] Whether constructed or in-born, the diversity of these people does not go unnoticed to any observer and has, in fact, become a critical socio-political issue from the colonial period till today. Mveng summarises the situation as follows: *At the end of this brief inquiry on the settlement of our country, the conclusion can be summarized in one word: diversity. Nothing in the past seemed to have prepared these peoples to become one people…Obviously, human Africa has decided to meet in our home and in the paradox of this little triangle as multiple as a continent, it is the entire Africa, surprised to live its unity with countless faces.*[202] Sudanese and Bantu people, therefore, had nothing in common and had found themselves within the national triangle that forms the territory of the Republic of Cameroon. Other diversity elements that could be added to the geographical and demographic factors are the English-Speaking World and the French-Speaking World inherited from European imperialism. Hence, David Tiomajou notes that: *"Cameroon is one of the most heterogeneous nations in Africa with regard to its local languages and ethnic groups. "*[203] Throughout the history of Cameroon and beyond, these in-born or constructed identities resulted in several ethnic groups that the Cameroon modern state

---

[200] Le Vine, Victor T.: The Cameroon Federal Republic, Cornelle University Press, London, 1971, p.2

[201] Obenga, Théophile: Les Bantu Langues-Peuples-Civilisations. Présence Africaine, 1985, p.91–107 ; Mveng, Engelbert: Histoire du Cameroun. CEPER, Yaoundé 1984, p.252–254 ; Warnier, Jean Pierre: « Archéologie et Histoire, Cameroun: le cas de l'Ouest », Communication présentée à la semaine de l'Histoire, Université de Yaoundé, avril 1981, texte dactylographié de 16 pages

[202] Mveng, Engelbert: op.cit. p.262–263

[203] Tiomajou, David: Language and Languages in Cameroon, A Diachronic View in: Breitinger, Eckhard: Defining News Idioms and Alternative Forms of Expression, Cross/Culter, 23, Amsterdam-Atlanta, 1996 p.251

used as the foundation of the same people and the same united and indivisible Nation.

## Strategic and Conflicting Groups

As stated earlier, there is no unanimity on the exact number of ethnic groups in Cameroon. Most of the literature uses fundamental criteria such as languages, cultures and other common history to count ethnic groups. For the proponents of this literature, in Cameroon, there are as many ethnic groups as there are linguistic communities that share the same cultural and historical legacy. Obviously, they all fell in the trap that Theophile Obenga calls *colonial ethnology*[204] whose single aim was to use a pseudo-scientific approach to demonstrate how too different Africans are from one another, thus paving the way to the colonizer who would easily divide and conquer the continent.

However, without being a specialist in comparative linguistics, some effort on observation, in this regard, provides a totally different ethnographic landscape in Cameroon with groups of population in *major linguistic areas* resulting from the two Bantu and Sudanese[205] metalanguages which are spoken everywhere on the Cameroonian territory certainly with varying nuances between communities, but which do not turn them into languages different from one another in terms of a *language as a system* according to the Swiss linguist, Ferdinand de Saussure.[206] If, in addition to this we consider sociopolitical and historical indicators as for instance, quotas of the fair political regional balance *(équilibre regional)*, ethno-regional origins of various governments of Cameroon since 1958 and of the 100 most influential men and women of Cameroon, we will realize that Cameroon does not have 250 ethnic groups with clear-cut inflexible social boundaries. There are a much reduced number of conflicting social aggregates whose community consciousness has been built throughout the politi-

---

[204] Obenga, Théophile: op.cit.

[205] Three of the four language families, in Africa, are in Cameroon: the Afro-Asiatic, Nilo-Saharan and Niger-Congo. The Bantu and Sudanese metalanguages are derivatives from the Niger-Congo family.

[206] Ferdinand, De Saussure: *Écrits de linguistique générale* (éd. par Simon Bouquet; Rudolf Engler, Antoinette Weil), Paris: Gallimard, 2002

cal, economic and social development of Cameroon that must be taken into account in every sector of the management of public affairs.

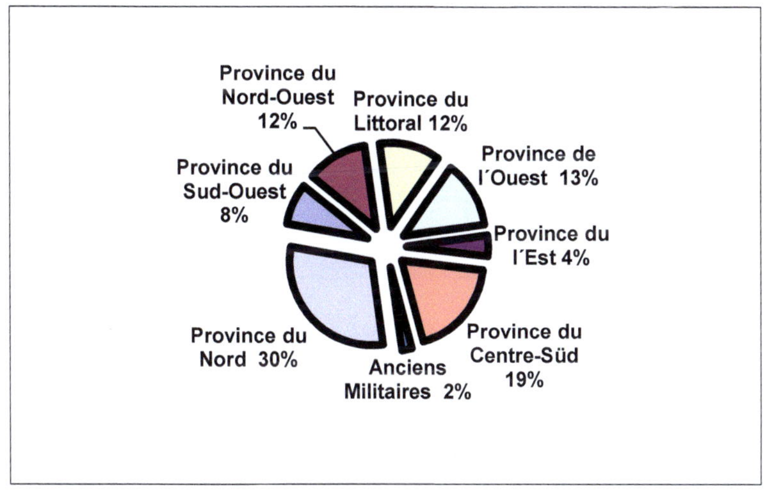


***Chart 1:****Political quotas of ethno-regional balance determined by province byDecreeN°82-407 of September 7th 1982, amending and supplementing certain provisions of decree N° 75-496 of July 3rd 1975 establishing a general policy of Administrative competitive exams in the United Republic of Cameroon.. Source: Tagou (2006).*

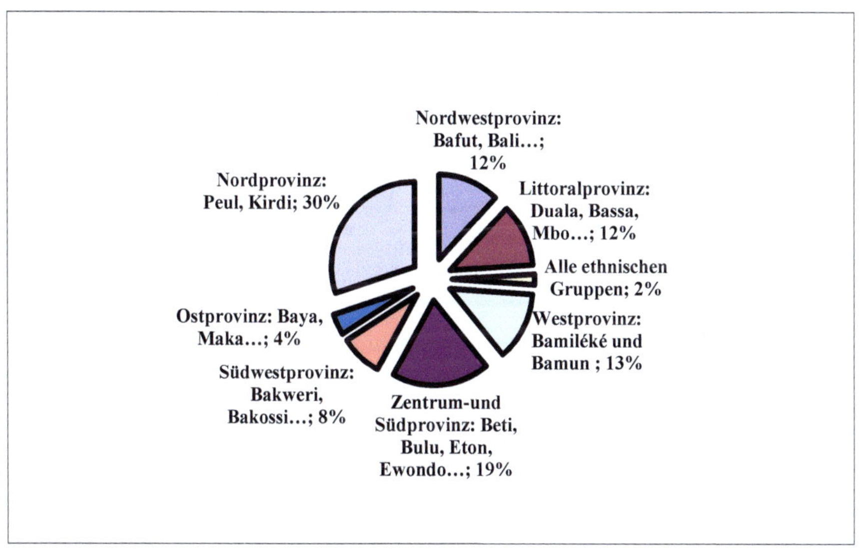


***Chart 2:*** *Ethno-regional interpretation of regional balance quotas. Source: Tagou (2006).*

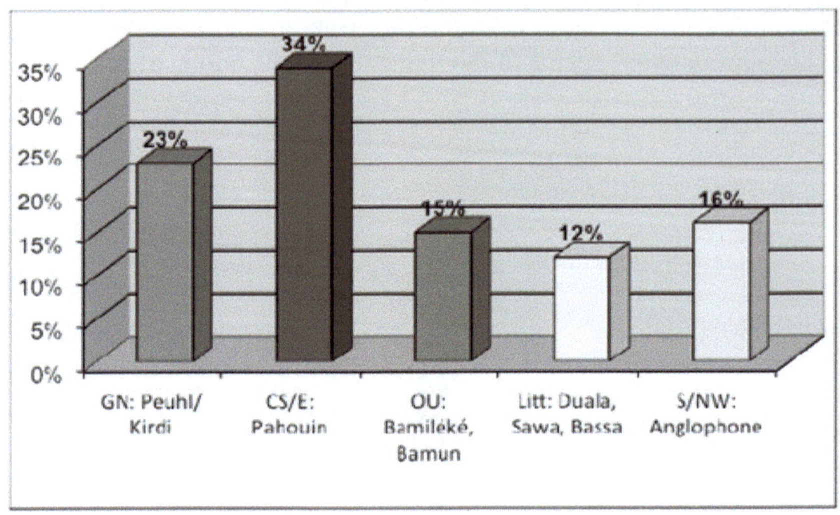



*Flow chart1: Distribution by province of origin of holders of ministerial positions in different governments from 1958 to 2006. Source: Tagou (2006).*[207]

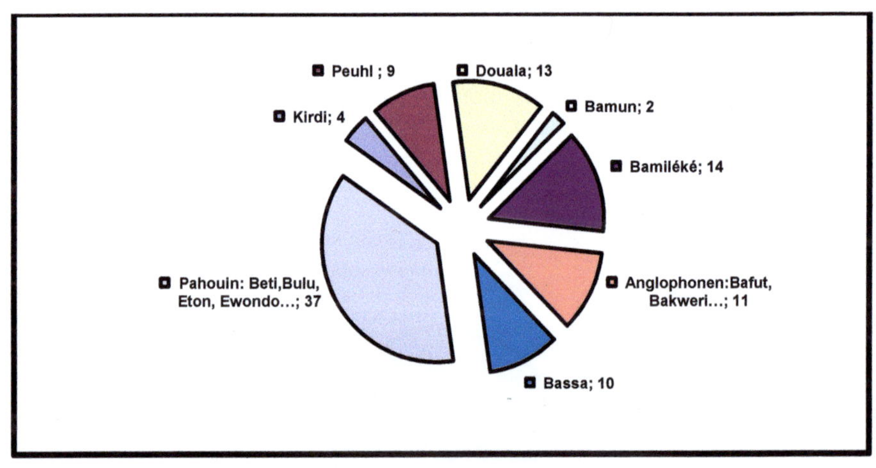



**Chart3:** *Regional origin of 100 most influential men and women in academia, economics, politics, civil administration and the military in Cameroon. Source: Tagou (2006).*

---

[207] It should be noted that Anglophone (S/NW) is not a tribe or an ethnic group per se. Many tribes or ethnic groups of the same linage have settled in the Southwest as well as in Littoral regions; in Northwest as well as in West and the Central regions of Cameroon. Some details on the overlapping settlement of population amongst administrative regions in Cameroon are presented later in this work.

With regard to the statistical data in flow charts and charts above, it is clear that there are not 250 conflicting groups as the scary atomizing rationale of *colonial ethnology* would have wished, but quite on the contrary, only **7+1 Conflicting and Strategic Groups** whose level of participation in and exclusion from the distribution and management of state resources can cause frustration to the extent of jeopardizing Cameroon territorial and political integrity and sovereignty. These groups are **the Pahouin** (the Bulu/Beti socio-politically speaking) of the Center, the South and the East; **the Bamilike** (also known as Grass-field) of the West; **the Fulbe** or Fulani (known as Northerners) of the Adamawa, the North and the Far North; **the Sawa** (or the Duala and others) of the Littoral; **the Bassa** of the Littoral and the Center; **the Bamoun** of the West; **the Kirdi** of the Far North; **the Anglophones** (who represent 1 in the formulae 7+1) of the North-West and the South-West. It is on the same line of atomized vision of the Cameroon ethnic landscape that Andreas Mehler states that: *"Ethnicity has also been viewed as a potentially significant source of conflict...Out of some two hundred small ethnic communities which had once existed there emerged larger groupings shaped by a variety of forces."*[208] Historical, political, cultural, economic, strategic and religious bases of potential threats and destabilization of these 7+1 groups have been amply discussed elsewhere.[209] From the history of Cameroon and according to the conceptual framework of our analysis, the Fulbe group was strategic from 1958 to 1982 and from 1982 to present; it is the Pahouin group that has the executive power. The up-date of the 2006 data would provide the same pattern today of the ethno-regional set up of the socio-political reality of Cameroon.[210]

---

[208] Mehler, Andreas: Cameroun and the politics of patronage, in: David Birmingham/Phyllis M. Martin (Hrsg.): History of Central Africa. The contemporary years since 1960, London/New York 1998, S.48.

[209] Tagou, Célestin: op.cit. 69–81

[210] The current political, economic, academic administrative and military highest officials (September 2017) are as follows: **President of the Republic** (Paul Biya, Pahouin) ; **President of the Senate** (Marcel Niat Njifenji, Bamiléke) ; **Prime Minister** (Philemon Yang, Anglophone) ; **President of the National Assembly** (Djibril Cavaye Yeguie, Fulani) ; **Main Presidents of political opposition parties**: (SDF: John Frudi, Anglophone; UNPD: Bello Bouba Maïgari, Fulani ; UDC: Adamou Ndam Njoya, Bamoun ; UPC:

**Strategic Groups**

As defined above, strategic groups are those at the central power, that is, the group from which, the President of the Republic is a native. Hence in the case of Cameroon, two groups have been strategic since independence, namely; the Fulani and the Pahouin. Fulani had this position until 1982 when President Amadou Ahidjo handed over the position of the President of the Republic to his constitutional successor, Paul Biya. From this moment, the Fulani lost the central power and were relegated to the periphery of the power to the profit of Pahouin.

*The Pahouin (Bulu/Beti) Strategic Group*

In an analysis of the socio-economic factors of the UPC establishment in various regions of Cameroon, political scientist, Joseph Richard has noted that *in the 19th century, the Beti-Pahouin migration towards the South beyond Sanaga river led to the creation of quite spread zone…Owing to the military value of the first elements of this migration and to the superior number of migratory waves over the people that the Pahouin met, it could be considered that all the population of the region is made up of Pahouins or Pahouinized.*[211] The Pahouin ethnonym refers to the various Bantu tribes that, following several migratory waves. They settled in the current regions of the Center, the South and the East of Cameroon, and had no political connotation. However, the replacement term, Bulu/Beti has a strong

---

Bapooh Lipot, Bassa ; MDR: Dakole Daissala, Kirdi ; MRC: Maurice Kamto, Bamiléké); **Minister of Economy, Planning and Regional Development** (Ousmane Alamine Mey, Fulani) ; **Minister of Justice** (Laurent Esso, Sawa) ; **Ministre of Defense** (Joseph Beti Assomo, Pahouin) ; **Delegate to The National Security** (Martin Mbarga Nguéle, Pahouin) ; **Secretary of State in Charge of the Gendarmerie** (Etoga Galaxe, Pahouin) ; State Universities' **Rectors:** Yaounde I University: (Maurice Aurelien Sosso, Sawa) ; Yaoundé II University (Minkoa Shé, Pahouin) ; University of Dschang (Tsafack Nanfosso, Bamiléké) ; University of Maroua (Idrisou Alioum, Fulani) ; University of Douala (François Xavier Etoa, Pahouin) ; University of Buea (Ngomo Horace Manga, Pahouin) ; University of Ngaoundéré (Uphie Chinje Florence, Anglophone) ; University of Bamenda (Teresa Nkuo Akenji, Anglophone).**Wealthiest Cameroonians according to Forbes 2016 ranking**: Baba Ahmadou Danpullo (Fulani); Paul Fokam Kammogne (Bamiléke), Famille Muketé (Anglophone)…

[211] Joseph, Richard: Le mouvement nationaliste au Cameroun. Ed. Karthala, 1986 p.142

socio-political dimension which has come very much into focus in discussions on ethnicity with regard to political integration and resources' sharing in Cameroon since 1982. Referring to the same groups of Cameroonian population, Mbuyinga assigns the phrase *the Bantu of the Equator* to the Fang, the Eton, the Ewondo, the Mvele, the Lepek, the Mengang, the Eki, the Bane, the Make, the Bulu....[212] The strategic role that falls on this group of Cameroonian population goes further back to the German colonial period. Charles Atangana, the chief translator (German-Ewondo) won the respect of German colonizers who found in him a reliable partner in the negotiation with the local populations. He was, thus, appointed senior traditional leader of the Ewondo and the Bane.[213] The position of the Ewondo and Bane senior traditional leader became one of the historical benchmarks of the ethnic identity construction process in this region of Cameroon. Other induced effects of the German colonial period that proved to be positively constitutive factors of the socio-political weight and importance of the Pahouin in independent Cameroon were, on the one hand, the facts that "Jaunde" town was chosen as the final capital city after the towns of "Duala" and Buea; and on the other hand, the education and training of the first elite of the country in institutions set up by colonizers and the church. These historical prerequisites pave the way to the ascension of a son of the soil to the high office in 1982 and will make a major contribution to the consolidation of ethnic awareness in terms of *Us and You, the included and the excluded.* Total political and military power control in Yaoundé city and even the country becomes a significant factor in the strategy of the group to monopolize political power and remain in charge of sharing the country's resources. This group's political awareness and ethnic identity have further developed with three socio-political events that Cameroon has witnessed namely: the 1984 aborted military coup; the 1990s radicalization of democratic claims and indiscriminate charges made against the Bulu/Beti group as being solely responsible for the political disintegration of the country; the rampant

---

[212] Mbuyinga, Elenga: op.cit.p.83

[213] Mehler, Andreas: Kamerun in der Ära Biya: Bedingungen, erste Schritte und Blockaden einer demokratischen Transition. IAK, Hamburg, 1993, p.79

corruption, nepotism and all the cycles of economic and social crisis that Cameroon has undergone since then. Seen as the scapegoat for all the ills of the country, the group finds in the reviving of their identity, strengthening of their ethnic links, appealing to mechanic solidarity and political power monopolization as the only strategies for protection, defense and survival. It is in this line that Charly Gabriel Mbock notes that: *the construction of the Bulu-Beti ethnic fact is taking place on a poly-ethnicity that henceforth finds legitimacy in the self-defense logic linked to maintaining the power that the Anglo-Bami want to snatch and beyond to the protection of advantages of the corrupt state.*[214] However, it is not fair to place all the blame on the Bulu-Beti ethnic group for being solely responsible for all the socio-political and economic difficulties of Cameroon. Some of the fierce critics of governance of the regime are natives of the Bulu-Beti group.[215] In addition, note has to be taken of the fact that a good number of other periphery groups' elite are, indeed, associated in a crony way to their counterparts of the Center, South and East regions in the mismanagement of the country and are, in fact, partly significantly responsible for the country's bad governance. Despite all this, it is obvious in the popular perception that most of the political power is in the hands of the Pahouin. *Jeune Afrique* special envoy summarizes it as follows: *Power...belongs to the South, President Paul Biya's native region that, fast speakers like to refer to, not without sarcasm, as* **the organizing country;** *and where the Bulu form the majority.* President Paul Biya is Bulu and *today, biases have not changed in the minds of those who are fighting against the regime. A Fang, Beti or Bulu opponent will always be suspected of secretly mingling with the power.*[216]With the Presidency of the Republic since 1982, the Bulu-Beti ethnic group is at the central power and, thus, meets the conditions and criteria for the Strategic Group in Cameroon. In this capacity, this strategic group pulls other groups of the

---

[214] Mbock, Charly Gabriel ed.: Les conflits ethniques au Cameroun: Quelles sources, quelles solutions ? Sep et Saagraph, Yaoundé, 2000, p.54

[215] This is actually the case of Dieudonné Essomba, of late Jean Marc Ela and Mongo Béti

[216] Dougueli, Georges in: op.cit. p.34–39

Center, East and South as they share the same cultural matrix and the same Bantu meta-language.

## Conflicting Groups

If the Strategic Group is at the central power, then the conflicting ones are at the periphery. They are loitering around the Strategic Group waiting for the best opportunity to take the power. They use either rebels or democratic opposition to challenge the political hegemony of the Strategic Group. Its elite is generally divided between those connected to the central power, and who are helping the Strategic Group to consolidate its positions while taking advantage of annuities and those who are criticizing and protesting. In the case of Cameroon, there are seven distinctive groups that along the history of the county have built identity references that today demonstrate the difference between *Us and You*, between *the in-groups* and *the out-groups*.

### *The Fulbe/Fulani and the Kirdi*

According to our analytical framework of SG/CG, the **Fulbe/Fulani**[217]had the strategic position from the independence of Cameroon to 1982 when President Amadou Ahidjo, a Fulani native gave the presidential seat to his constitutional successor, Paul Biya. Despite the fact that the Fulani have settled a bit everywhere on the national territory, their native soil stretches from the Adamawa region to the Far North of the country, including the North. The terms Greater-North *(Grand Nord)* and the Northern part *(Septentrion)* are the political references of these three administrative regions and are often used when the distribution of resources between elite members and larger groups is at stake at the national level. The socio-religious set-up of their traditional communities in Lamidats based on the Muslim religion and the position that this group has had in the political history of Cameroon is the basis of their socio-economic influ-

---

[217] In the Greater North, Fulani are associated to Hausa and Kanuri. The nuance between the three social aggregates is that Fulani have the political power, Hausa are business people and the kanuri are custodians of traditions and customs, the pure bred Muslim culture.

ence and their political weight on the national scene. The Fulani hegemony also has historical roots that go back into the history of this region. As a matter of fact, on behalf of the Jihad led by the Muslim reformist Usmane Dan Fodio, the native populations of the current Greater-North were submitted to the dominance of the Fulani's nobility and the Muslim culture, thus, became the social model in the entire region. It is at this time that the term **Kirdi** took a socio-political connotation as a degrading qualification for all the non-Muslim people of the region.[218] In order to escape this tendency of Fulbe assimilation, several Kirdi people opted for Christianity in all its doctrinal versions. Bororos are also part of the Fulani and the practice of pastoral nomadization compelled them to spread and settled right to the current North-West and West regions of the country.

In the present Cameroon, migrant or settled citizens, native of the Greater-North, show a group awareness carried by the elite that were mostly built up under Amadou Ahidjo's regime. With the fair policy of regional balance, Ahidjo facilitated the social progress of several natives of the Greater-North who became dignitaries of political life in all sectors and at the national level. From the various cabinets to the army, including all sectors of public administration, from 1966 until his resignation in 1982, Ahidjo entrusted important ministerial and administrative positions to Fulani. He equally promoted the development of powerful economic operators, native of the Greater-North. As in the past, Fulani remained owners of large agriculture and cattle farms in the entire Greater-North and even the North-West of Cameroon. They are also well-known in transportation and real estate. Two of the top ten wealthiest Cameroonians are of Fulani origin and one of the two takes the first place as the wealthiest in the entire francophone Africa.[219] Like the Bamoun of the West region,

---

[218] The concept Kirdi has a negative connotation from the onset and is used to refer commonly to the entire spectrum of non-Muslim population groups: the Toupouri, the Tikar, the Mofou, the Mandara, the Giziga, the Boum, the Baya, the Bété, the Ndi, etc.

[219] They are Baba Danpullo and Nana Bouba. Refer to:
http://www.cotedivoire.news/actualite/8650-top-10-hommes-plus-riches-cameroun-2017.html et https://www.voaafrique.com/a/les-30-plus-grosses-fortunes-d-afrique-francophone-pesent-10-milliards-de-dollars-selon-forbes-afrique/3620354.htmlconsulted on 07/09/2017 at 12h30

they enjoy a very high influence in Muslim settings of all forms and not only in their native regions but in all the country and mostly in large towns.

The change in power in 1982 shook the Fulani hegemony in the region and nationwide when Paul Biya's new regime diversifies allies in the region by promoting a native of Kirdi. This readjustment of allies will take a tragic turn with the aborted coup of April 6 to 8, 1984 in which several Fulani dignitaries (Ministers and senior Army officials) were involved. It is in this line that Jean Njoya writes: *Ties were immediately broken following a plot attributed to the Fulani supporters of the former head of State. It is, then that the Kirdi found their way into a political representation with the appointment of Ayan Luc, a Christian from the Toupouri sub-group and the destruction of the Northern bloc with the creation policy of new administrative units....Evidently, President Biya has found a source of support against the Muslim-Fulani bloc that had sympathized with former President Ahidjo during the 1983–1984 double-headed crisis.*[220] Despite reducing the Fulani group to a political minority, to the benefit of kirdi by President Paul Biya's regime from 1984, the Fulani political weight and influence remained and still are an indisputable and unavoidable geo-cultural and geo-political fact in the calculation of great balance and socio-political stability of Cameroon. President Paul Biya's regime would not completely get rid of them in the management of the country. Political figures such as Sadou Hayatou, Bello Bouba Maigari, Ousmane Mey, Issa Tchirouma, Marafa Yaya Hamidou etc. are still part of the officials of Biya's regime until the breakup with some following the anti-corruption fight with "sparrow hawk operation"*(operation épervier)*. At the sport level, a Fulani son, Issa Hayatou brought honor to Cameroon as head of the African Football Confederation for 29 years with a remarkable tenure at the head of FIFA.

It is important to remember that with democratic openness in the 1990s, the non-Muslim natives of the Northern part of Cameroon

---

[220] Jean: Démocratisation, divergences ethniques et politisation de la pluralité au Cameroun in *Canadian Journal of African Studies,* 36 (2002) 2, p.249

who were claiming their autonomy mobilize themselves around a movement called *Kirditude*[221] to reverse the crony relationship that the Greater-North region had until then with the central power in Yaoundé. The Kirditude movement was supported by Jean Baptiste Baskouda, Dakolé Daissala among others.

The group's awareness of these populations of the Greater-North was once more articulated with the outbreak of the Boko Haram crisis in which their elite were accused by the Lekie appeal signed in particular by Henri Eyebe Ayissi accusing the Northerners of being *Boko Haram accomplices notably in the Northern regions and the strategy of encouraging the division of the national territory*. Feeling clearly targeted, the dignitaries of the Northern region of Cameroon reacted immediately through one of the most authoritative voices on the Cameroonian political scene, who condemned the allegations of the center region and warned against their attempt to turn Cameroon into *Rwanda*.[222] It is important to recall that besides separatist claims of SCNC,[223] literature on Cameroonian politics had not had this type of polarization especially in a war where soldiers are dying at the battle front. The socio-political animosity between ethnic groups had never crossed the lines of negative and reductionist biases from one another and vice versa, to become a pitched battle between the elite while the republican army is at the war zone against an elusive enemy. The political opposition and the party in power have often and mutually blamed one another in different circumstances with regard to the

---

[221] As the "négritude" and "tigritude", groups pejoratively referred to by the term Kirdi own the concept stripping it of its negative connotation and turning it into an identity that bring them pride that they want to express at the national political level. Reference: https://www.researchgate.net/publication/281747574_Kirditude_Ideologie_de_la_major ite_opprimee_au_Cameroun checked on 28/09/2017

[222] Reacting to this appeal of August 31st 2014, the Elite of the Greater North in a press release read by the President of the national Assembly, Cavaye Yeguie Djibril who violently denounced the stigmatization that was victimizing them.

[223] SCNC: Southern Cameroonian National Council is the managing committee of the SCPC (Southern Cameroon People Conference), a secessionist movement created in 1994 in Bamenda by some Anglophone elite; a part of which has been claiming the existence of a certain Republic of Ambazonia since August 31st 2006. We will come back to it later when we present the 7+1 of the 8 strategic and conflicting groups in Cameroon.

management of the affairs of the Cameroon State, but it was the first time that officials of the same party, the CPDM had broken up direct dialogue and used the media to denounce and reject the complicity of their party comrades facing one of the most dangerous threats that Cameroon had ever witnessed.

In a caricatured manner, the authors of the Lekie statement are Christians of the Pahouin Strategic Group and those that replied are in the majority Muslims and Fulani of the Northern part of Cameroon.[224] The recent history of potential conflicts on the African continent and in Eastern Europe show how, it is through little media and reported accusations that civil war started in Kosovo, in Rwanda, in Ivory Coast, in Sudan, in CAR, in DRC etc. When the same people communicate through the media, it is the beginning of the breakup of dialogue which is, in fact, a true keystone of mutual understanding and acceptance, of tolerance necessary for social cohesion.

This means that the Fulani and Kirdi[225] of the Northern part of Cameroon form a group whose concept of Greater-North can link their two religious civilizations, and that the Yaoundé regime needs to work with for political stability and Positive Peace.

*The Sawa*

Also called *Coastal Bantu*, the Sawa were the first Cameroonians to have contact with European explorers, slave traders and later with colonizers. Owing to their geographical position on the Atlantic coast, the Sawa were at first, at the heart of the relationships between German colonizers and the Cameroon hinterland before being subsequently sidelined during the total conquest of Kamerun.[226] This historical heritage, coupled with their privileged geographical position,

---

[224] Tagou, Célestin in: African Journal of Peace Communication and Development Vol.002, Nov.2016, pp.7–9

[225] It should be noted that there is a change in the perception of the majority notion in the Northern part of Cameroon. Here the demographic majority is Kirdi and the political and economic majority is Fulani and they are both in competition. Reference: Tagou, Célestin in: Gwoda Adder & al. (sd.) op.cit.: pp.35–49

[226] Yenshu Vebo, Emmanuel: Levels of Historical Awarness. The Development of Identity and Ethnicity in Cameroon in: Cahiers d'Etudes africaines, 43 (2003) P.610

served as the first humus for the development of the Sawa ethnic group awareness in Cameroon. This is noticed by Austin and Merrick when they state: *"The Duala/Sawa became aware of themselves as a group with a history of interposition between European and the rest of Cameroon."*[227] These historical and geographical advantages placed the Sawa people and their region far ahead of other regions and people of Cameroon. Hence, the first largest seaport, the first largest airport in Cameroon and the sub-region were built in Douala, which is not only the head of the region, but also the first major financial hub of Cameroon and Central African sub-region. Historical leading figures such as Rudolf Duala Manga Bell, Alexandre Duala Manga Bell, Rev. Adolphe Lotin'a Same, King Akwa, Paul Soppo Priso, and Laurent Esso etc., who each at his/her time made the history of Cameroon, equally contributed to strengthen the sense of belonging between the Sawa. Hence, from the colonial power to the two regimes that Cameroon has had, the Sawa have always been taken into consideration in the sharing of resources. Geography and history gave them this asset that they can put on the scale at the national political level: *On the other hand, it should be noted, as it is a significant point in the analysis of Cameroonian politics after 1945, that despite the demographic weakness of the Douala and the massive arrival of immigrants from the hinterland to the seaport, they perfectly knew how to preserve a significant political power.*[228] The Sawa have demonstrated it on several occasions when they felt that they were not taken into consideration. This was the case in 1996 following council elections when the *Sawa movement* brought together the political elite of the Littoral, the South-West and the South to protest against the political dominance of Bamileke in the town of Douala: *"In 1996 when the Grand Sawa Movement was formed, linking the elites of South West, Littoral and Southern Provinces...the ambition of the promotors of Sawa led them to float the idea of the Grand Sawa political party stretching from Campo to Mamfé."*[229]

---

[227] Austen and Derrick (199) Ibid. p.610

[228] Joseph, Richard op.cit. p.35

[229] Nyamnjoh, Francis/Rowlands, Michael.: Elite Association and the Politics of Belonging in Cameroon, in *African affairs* (1998), 3, p.331–332

Aware of the cultural unity of the Atlantic coast people from Campo to Mamfe, the elite saw in this great *Pansawa* organization, mobilizing all the coastal people to support Paul Biya's political action, the only means of protection against the dominance of the immigrants from the West and the North-West.

In Cameroon, therefore, Sawa can be relied on not only because of the historical and geographical heritage, but also because of their culture and food. Beyond the canoe, the traditional broom, the Ngondo, the Makossa and Ndole have become very well-known cultural and national values even abroad.

*The Bassa*

The Bassa are an ethnic group whose identity awareness has no doubt in Cameroon. From the historical point of view, the Bassa are among the ethnic groups that underwent various forms of colonial oppression during the conquest and the exploitation of *Kamerun* hinterland. They experimented in their flesh and mind, forced labor atrocities in the construction of the railway between Duala and Jaunde (MittelKamerun), which permitted the German colonizers to exploit its colony's wealth (Grosskamerun) established by the sharing at the Berlin Conference of 1884/1885. Beyond the suffering that they underwent under the German colonial period, the Bassa also made political history in Cameroon through resistance against any form of colonial dominance. **Ruben Um Nyobe**, the leading figure and executive secretary of the very first political party in Cameroon, is a native of Bassa ethnic group. This political commitment and fight for the independence and the reunification of Cameroon have made him a national hero. With recent studies carried out by Thomas Deltombe & al, the scope of the human tragedy that took place in silence in the Sanaga-Maritime pacification zone (PACZO) can be a little more appraised. Sandwiched in what Achille Mbembe calls *…the tragic combination liberation war/anti-protestation war and civil war…* Bassa's ancestors paid a high price for giving birth to a son whose nationalism shook the lines of the revolutionary war philosophy of the French Chief, Colonel Jean Lamberton. Between 1957 and 1958, Jean Lamberton and his team *… conducted a block-by-*

*block grid of the territory divided in neighborhoods and sub-
neighborhoods, deporting people to resettlement camps, mobilizing
battle militia, extrajudicial killings, psychological influence, forced
disappearances, torture...* It is in these waves of pacification opera-
tions that **Um Nyobe** the Cameroonian (or Kamerunischer) leader
was murdered on September 13th 1958 and his body was desecrat-
ed.[230]

Despite the rallying of some elite members of the Bassa ethnic group
to the two political regimes that Cameroon has had since independence (Mayi Matip with Ahidjo and Kodock with Biya) and the regional balance policy that has contributed to the development of several Bassa elite, in the political circles of the two regimes, the Bassa
people always feel that they are the losers of Cameroon's independence. At another level, the Bassa have also built a high profile around
football, a major sport activity in Cameroon. Legendary football
players such as Roger Milla, Joseph Antoine Bell, and Samuel Eto'o
to mention a few have made all Cameroonians proud beyond Bongo
Shobi, Assiko and other Mbobock legends.

The Bassa, therefore, form a group which is a potential threat with
regard to our conceptual framework of Strategic and Conflicting
Groups and they must be taken into consideration in political games
and stakes in Cameroon.

*The Bamoun*

The Bamoun ethnic group shares the West region with the Bamileke
ethnic group. The political weight of the Bamoun on the Cameroun
national scene is the result of several historical, cultural and political
factors. The invention of a writing system, architectural knowledge
demonstrated in the construction of the royal palace in Foumban, the
design and production of a priceless royal throne[231] by Bamoun

---

[230] Deltombe, Thamas & al.: La guerre du Cameroun: l'invention de la Françafrique, La
Découverte, Paris 2016.p.13, pp.120–125

[231] King Njoya was the inventor of the Bamoun Writing system and his prestigious throne
is exhibited at the Dahlemdorf Museum in Berlin allegedly donated to Guillaume II as a
birthday gift.

sculptors are among other heritage assets that the entire Cameroon owes to the Bamoun people. The Bamoun have one of the oldest dynasties that have existed in Sub-Saharan Africa before the various waves of slavery and imperialist violence. If several Bamoun kings have collaborated with the various colonial powers and the two regimes of Yaoundé have always sought and obtained the political support of the royal court, that does not conceal the historical fact of a Bamoun son's nationalism, Dr. Roland Moumie, who was the president of the Cameroon People Union (CPU) and who failed to survive in Geneva on November 3rd 1960 after being poisoned.[232]In return for this policy of being close to the various powers in place, the Bamoun have always had one of their worthy sons in the power structures, and some are still being talked about years after they have retired from administrative and political life. It is the case of Ndam Njoya, former Minister of Education and the late legendary director of Secret Services of Cameroon' Jean Forchive, whose service to the nation made history in the country. Today, the Bamoun are an example of transcendence and transformation of mega-conflicts (conflicts of civilization) between Christians and Muslims in Cameroon.[233] And even if today the council of Foumban town is in the hands of *Cameroon Democratic Union*, constant communication and affinity are always being well forged between the *Etoudi Palace* and that of Foumban.

*The Bamileke*

The Conflicting Group that has historically remained at the heart of post-independence political crisis in Cameroon is the Bamileke ethnic group. This group, which shares the native Western region with the Bamoun is made up of about one hundred kingdoms, (chiefdoms) whose common cultural matrix is the initiation rite of the kings and dignitaries called *La'akem*. Here we have a typical example of

---

[232] Thomas Deltombe & al. explain the poisoning episode of Felix Roland Moumie by a secret agent of the French SDECE called William Bechtel. Op.cit.: pp.184–187

[233] Mbouombouo, Pierre & Ntchoutizo, Flore: Cohabitation musulmans/chrétiens dans le Noun au Cameroun: Exemple de posture préventive et résiliente aux risques de conflits religieux et idéologiques au Cameroun in *Revue Africaine de Paix, Communication et Développement,* vol.002 Novembre 2016 pp139–159

ethnonyms constructed from scratch. The concept *Bamileke*, in fact, has no significance in the various dialects spoken by the population of this region of Cameroon. Delaroziere clearly states on this point: *The term Bamileke does not match with any native or racial descrip-tion. It is unknown to almost all the people concerned...*[234] The most likely origin of this ethnonym that has prevailed in the ethnographic and socio-political vocabulary of Cameroon is the one indicated by the geographer, Jean Louis Dongmo. According to him, the word Bamileke comes from a phonetic mispronunciation of the phrase Bali *"Mba Lekeo"*[235] by the German explorer Zingraff. He was, thus re-ferring to the populations of the current Menoua and Bamboutos di-visions who have settled at the foot of Bamboutos Mountain follow-ing several migratory waves. The Bamileke are from Sudanese Tikar origin. The word Bamileke appears for the first time in the report by the German commander of the Mbo station in 1905.[236]It referred un-til 1947 to populations different from the Bangwa, the Bafeng, and the Bafum etc. Its transposition as a generic ethnonym for all the populations of this region certainly remains unclear, but it has gained ground as identity concept according to the historical development and political events since the German colonial period until the first decade of Cameroon independence. Jean Lamberton ended the de-bate in the following terms: *the explanation is plausible; its accuracy matters less: today for francophone Cameroonians and for most of the other people Bamileke are Bamileke...*[237] If Bamileke are Bamileke, in what way does their awareness of a distinctive group with regard to identity inclusion and exclusion make of them one of the conflicting groups with a real potential threat in Cameroon and which furthermore scares other groups? In the literature, there are

---

[234]  R. Delaroziere in Mbuyenga, Elenga: op.cit. p.48

[235]  Replying to a question from Zingraff who wanted to know what they called the popula-tions with impressive agricultural skills residing at the foot of Bamboutos Mountain, the Bali porter told him that they were called the "Mba Lekoe" (the people of the bottom) Reference: Dongmo, Jean-Louis: Le Dynamisme Bamiléké (Cameroun), Yaoundé 1981, pp10–11.

[236]  Deutsches Kolonialblatt XVI, 1905, p.501

[237]  Lamberton, Jean: Ibid. p.56

three basic answers to the question which are historical-political, economic and demographic.

From the history of Cameroon standpoint, in the most majority, the Bamileke region and its populations truly supported nationalist fights for independence and the reunification of Cameroon under the flag of Um Nyobe's Cameroon Population Union. If Dr. Roland Moumie, president of CPU was a native of the West but of the Bamoun ethnic group, Ernest Ouandié, Martin Singap, Momo Paul, Déléne Jérémie and other members of the ALNK[238] who carried on the independence fight underground in the Mungo and the West region up to the 1970s are indeed Bamileke. The continuation of the fight for independence in the Bamileke region led Chief Colonel Jean Lamberton to say that *Cameron is set on the independence track with a really uncomfortable stone in the shoe…this stone is the presence of an ethnic minority: the Bamileke…*[239] Thomas Deltombe & al. amply demonstrate that after the Sanaga Maritime pacification that it was the Bamileke region that became the real demonstration ground for the Revolutionary War Philosophy (RWP). A systematic merciless warfare carried out in absolute silence, first, by the French colonial army and subsequently by proxy through the army of independent Cameroon. According to these authors, *after the 'Bassa', stigmatized during the PACZO movement, it is the 'Bamileke' who is literally on the grill.*[240] Described as *plague* by the then political police head, Jean Fochivé, *the terror policy…*[241] was applied to the letter in the Bamileke region between 1958 and 1970.[242] Terror hit its peak in this region where whole villages were burnt, women raped. Suspects were tortured and executed in public later beheaded and their heads exhibited in market squares to teach lessons to others. This complete

---

[238] The debate that opposes the proponents of the thesis of the continuation of the nationalist struggle in the Bamileke region (Mbuyinga Elenga,1989) and those of criminal and terrorist actions perpetrated by bunches of thieves and crooks (Bouopda Pierre Kamé, 2008) was brought to an end with the studies by Thomas Deltombe & al. (2011, 2016).

[239] Lambeton, Jean in Deltombe, Thomas &al., op.cit. p.175

[240] Ebid. p.175

[241] Deltombe, Thomas & al. Ibid. p.175

[242] Ibid. pp.201–204

warfare described by the Ahidjo's regime as detoxification and re-education campaign caused hundreds of thousands of deaths, and today gives rise to a controversy between the proponents of genocide thesis and those who think that it is a fantasy. Whatever the baseline analysis resulting from the opening of the historical archives announced by Francois Hollande in 2015, this dark episode of the history of Cameroon turned Bamileke into a group stereotyped with all kinds of negative biases. It is a dangerous and harmful group; should not be trusted and everything must be done to keep them out of the political power except for a few elite members compromised by France and Ahidjo's regime.[243]

This tragic episode of the political history of Cameroon compelled the Bamileke to develop a degree of phobia for the political affairs of the country and focused on business for which, nature has provided them with exceptional skills. Ahidjo's regime favorably guided them into that option in order to keep them a little bit away from politics. Hence, from the colonial period, the Bamileke focused more on small business, agriculture, bakery and other services such as transportation etc. They progressively rose and over the decades in the industry sector, large scale import/export, supermarkets, finance and banking, insurance and knowledge market. What Dongmo has described as *economic dynamism...that commands everyone's attention*[244] was equally noticed by Pierre Erny, who drew comparison between the Bamileke and the Tutsi of Rwanda. Pierre Erny noted that in *Cameroon, they talk a lot about Bamileke, a people of the mountains, characterized by highly structured chiefdoms...this ethnic group...is well-known for its busy activity in the economic life of the country and its special success in business and enterprises...it is often wondered where they get the dynamism from?*[245] Statistics from the 1980s testified this success of Bamileke in the economic sector: 58% of Cameroonians with import/export permits, 94% of land title

---

[243] A typical example is that of Samuel Kamé, one of the rare young intellectuals of that time who attended Sciences Po Paris l'ENFOM or the Bandjoun King, Joseph Kamga

[244] Dongmo, Jean-Louis: op.cit. p.9

[245] Erny, Pierre: Rwanda 1994 Clés pour comprendre le calvaire d'un peuple. L'Harmattan 1994, p.187

owners in major cities, 75% of cocoa traders, 47% of industrial production, 80% of taxi fleets and 59% of the informal sector were in the hands of Bamileke economic operators. Important business men such as Victor Fotso and Kadji Defosso[246] gained favors from the Ahidjo's regime.[247]Today, seven of the top ten wealthiest Cameroonians in business are Bamileke.[248] And according to the classification of the American magazine, Forbes two of them are among the top ten wealthiest French-speaking Africans.[249]

All sorts of socio-anthropological terms were used to justify Bamileke dynamism: the "tontine" system and attic tradition as indicators of being naturally inclined to saving, hardwork, tough, strict, traditionalist etc. But also greed, misers, bleak, wizard, cunning, *nfemlah, feyman* are clichés that Bamileke are labeled to positively or negatively legitimize their success in the economic sector in Cameroon. However, it should be stated that the hypertrophy carried out on the Bamileke dynamism hides another piece of socio-economic reality of this group tinted with precariousness, misery and poverty like several other Cameroonians from other ethnic groups. This other piece of reality is well socio-logically illustrated in the concept *the street smart Bamileke (le Débrouillard Bamileke)*. These street smart Bamileke are the ones that fill the unhealthy neighborhoods of large cities of the country such as Madagascar, Mokolo etc. in Yaoundé; New Bell, Bepanda, Village in Douala and that form a proletarian pool of cheap labor at the mercy of economic operators from the same ethnic group.

Demography is another basic factor of the Bamileke weight. The West region is one of the regions that have a heavy population density, with about 140 inhabitants per square kilometer in relation to the

---

[246] Mr Kadji Defosso passed away in August 2018

[247] Warnier, Jean Pierre: L'Esprit d'entreprise au Cameroun, Paris, Karthala 1993, p.5

[248] They are: Paul Fokam Kammogne, Samuel Foyou, Jean Samuel Noutchogouin, Sylvestre Ngouchinghe, Kate Fotso, Famille Sohaing, Joseph Kadji Defosso refer to: http://www.cotedivoire.news/actualite/8650-top-10-hommes-plus-riches-cameroun-2017.html of 07/09/2017

[249] They are Paul Fokam Kammogne who is 2nd in the ranking and Samuel Foyou who is in the 7th position.

national rate which is 39 inhabitants per square kilometer. This demographic pressure, coupled with zero sum succession system and the regional balance policy has greatly contributed to a strong migration of Bamileke to all parts in the Cameroon territory, in the sub-region and beyond. Since the colonial era, the first zones of Bamileke migration were the Mungo, the Littoral, the South-West and the Center. Progressively, they settled everywhere in Cameroon in search of new arable lands, conducive new roads and localities for business. At the national level, the Bamileke migrants are perceived as invaders and are at the heart of several crises based on the native/non-native dichotomy. The former are protesting their frustration towards the Bamileke multi-sector pre-dominance on their soil. One of the senior civil servants of the Ahidjo's regime, Felix Sabal Lecco stated on the eve of his death in 2010 that: *Those people are so numerous that one would say there are ants!-they are obliged to find ways to settle everywhere... is there any neighborhood that does not have Bamileke? Which village, which town does not have Bamileke in Cameroon? Not only in Cameroon, but everywhere worldwide! They are the Jews of Cameroon. One cannot avoid the Bamileke phenomenon. It is not possible. You cannot fight against the Bamileke phenomenon.*[250]

The analysis of this high ranking civil servant who, actively participated in the complete warfare to crush the last resistance squares of the Cameroon People Union nationalism in the Mungo and in the Bamilike land under Ahidjo, amply summarizes what has been established in the Cameroon political literature since that period: *the Bamileke problem or the Bamileke question.* Whether in Cameroon, a *Bamileke problem/a Bamileke question* exists or not, it is certain that from 1955 till today, the Bamileke model of integration with regard to acceptance and participation in all sectors and at all levels of the Cameroonian nation life is far from being a political normalcy. Cameroon history provides several episodes testifying the integration difficulties of Bamileke at the social, religious, academic, administrative, political levels and even in political opposition.[251] The Bamileke

---

[250] Deltombe, Thomas &al.: op.cit.p.205

[251] From Ahidjo's regime to that of Biya, we can cite the following conflict among others between the Bamileke and the Sawa, the Bulu, the Eton, the Mbo, the Bakweri, the

question leads to two types of feelings: the fear that others will lose all and the frustration of the Bamileke who feel excluded. Bamileke already have the economy and if they gain control of the politics, administration, academia, even the religion etc., what would be left to others? That is the Bamileke question today in Cameroon.

Beyond others' sense of fear that has evolved throughout the history of Cameroon, with episodes of xenophobic animosity, the Bamileke ethnic group carries a weight that every regime is aware of and has gone about developing its own generation of Bamileke followers.[252]

Hence, under Ahidjo there were leading figures such as: Enoch Kwayeb, Kamga Fokam, Sammuel Kamé, Paul Monthé, Jean Keutcha, Poufong Etienne Clément ... The Biya's regime in turn promoted new Bamileke political figures such as: Paul Tésa, Jean Kuete, Marcel Niat Njifendji, Tchouta Moussa, Augustin Kontchou Koumegni, Françoise Foning, Luc Sindjoun, Nganou Djoumessi among others. These are moderates that I described elsewhere in terms of *"softliners"* and who oppose *"hardliners"* that are found in shadowy cultural associations, Laakam, Binam etc...[253] The stock-in-trade of these associations is made up of denunciation, marginalization and injustice that only the Bamileke are victims of in Cameroon.[254]

---

Nyokon…, Court cases such as Victor Kanga, Ndongmo (1960–1970), Ethno-fascism controversies and de Mono-fascism of 1987 between Sindjoun Pokam and Mono Ndjana, mass up-rising against Bamiléke in the Catholic church (cases of Bishop Simo Gabriel in Douala in 1987 and Bishop André Wouking in Yaoundé in 1999). There is also the crisis within the SDF in 1995 and UNDP in 2002. For details on the difficult integration of Bamileke in Cameroon and the articulation of the Bamileke question, reference: Tagou, Célestin: op.cit. (2006) pp.143–197

[252] It is important to note here and that is relevant to all groups that, between the two regimes, the legitimacy of henchmen is progressively shifted from the top to the bottom, from the summit where the elite has been introduced and must be loyal to the bottom people who elect them thus providing them with some emancipating freedom in relation to the submit.

[253] Tagou, Célestin: op.cit. (2006) pp.88–89

[254] Laakam, the nebulous association sporadically attracts attention with very difficult to pin down memoranda and press releases from Shanda Tomne and Sindjoun Pokam,

*The Anglophones*

Owing to Cameroon's colonial history, in a span of 42 years that is from June 28th 1919 to October 1st 1960,[255] another identity reality, a reference to an exclusive feeling of *Us/You,* which has nothing to do with Africa and African culture, but rather connected to Shakespeare's language and culture, would emerge. If German possessions, Togoland and Kamerun had the same fate under the Society of Nations (1919–1946), with regard to the division and the sharing between the two victorious powers of the First World War, namely France and England, Cameroon's fate was more or less tragic towards the end of the United Nation trusteeship (1948–1961). During the 1956 referendum, the Western Togoland entirely joined the Gold Coast to form the current Ghana and the Eastern Togoland which became Togo under the leadership of the French West African (FWA) community. In the case of Cameroon, the June 1,1961, a referendum gave way to another constellation: the Northern part of the British Cameroon chose to join Nigeria and the Southern part, under John Ngu Foncha's guidance opted for its independence and joined the Republic of Cameroon. Both formed the Federal Republic of Cameroon on October, 1st 1961.[256] According to Koinings and Nyamnjoh, this date was the starting point of the famous "Anglophone problem" in Cameroon as they say *"The root of this problem may be traced back to 1961 when the political elites of the two territories with different colonial legacies – one French and the other British – agreed on the formation of a federal state…Gradually, this created an Anglophone consciousness: the feeling of being marginalised, exploited and assimilated by the francophone-dominated state,*

---

[255] When Germany lost the First World War, it was compelled to give up all its overseas belongings according to article 119 of the Versailles Treaty signed on June, 28th 1919. Of all German belongings in Africa, Togoland and Kamerun will undergo a special fate as they will be shared between France and England. Having already defeated the Germans in Togoland, French and the British shared Togoland in 1916 and Kamerun will face the same fate at the end of the war. This fate will be different at the independence period.

[256] Historical circumstances justify (English-French) bilingualism in the Republic of Cameroon which is an advantage with regard to Togo, 100% Francophone despite the national mourning day of July 1st 1960.

*and even by the francophone population as a whole.*"[257] It is important to know what this Anglophone consciousness consists in and to which extent it is different from the consciousness of other groups in Cameroon.[258]

The number **1** in the formulae **7+1** of the Strategic and Conflicting Groups that we have identified in Cameroon, therefore refers to this Conflicting Group whose exclusive identity reference is not African but rather the outcome of 42 years of identity construction based on a colonialist Western language and culture.[259] The Anglophone Conflicting Group refers to the population native of the South-West and North-West regions and not to all Cameroonians who speak English and master the British literature as well as poetry. The only identity element that Anglophone Cameroonians of these two regions have in common is the *colonial* linguistic and cultural legacy. We must admit that millions of young Cameroonians with Francophone parents are holders of GCE-A Level and have undertaken or are undertaking brilliant university studies in Anglo-Saxon academia in Cameroon, in England, in the USA, in Canada... They know English, have been moulded in the British culture and thus share the same *common heritage (education, culture, and way of life...)*[260] with Anglophones of the South-West and North-West. But they do not politically count among the Anglophone Cameroonians that constitute this Conflicting Group. It is also obvious that Cameroonians from the South-West and North-West regions educated in Francophone zone or who have a very good knowledge of Moliere's language and Culture are also not accepted by other Francophones and much more, they are seen

---

[257] Konings, Piet/Nyamnjoh, Francis B.: The Anglophone Problem in Cameroon, in *Journal of Modern African Studies,* 35 (1997) 2,. p.207

[258] Banseka, Cage:The Anglophone Problem in Cameroon: A Conflict Resolution Perspective in *African Renaissance* Vol. 3 No.2 March/April 2006, pp94–104

[259] The other 7 strategic or conflicting groups do not identify themselves in relation to the French language, but rather in relation to some patterns of African culture substrate specific to each group.

[260] David Tiomajou,to whom I owe the translation of this book from French to English, is a Francophone Cameroonian from Babadjou. My student Paul Beppe Yombo, who wrote and defended a brilliant master Thesis in the English language, last March, is a Francophone Cameroonian from Bafia.

and officially considered as Anglophones.[261] The English-speaking world is therefore a political credential seen from within as well as out of the concerned group. Besides this double-sided phenomenon, there is a generation of Cameroonian children of 21st century resulting from the two sides and who are perfectly bilingual owing to maternal and basic education and even secondary education, new trends and guidance that several Cameroonian primary, middle and high schools offer.[262] We wonder what these children will become: *Anglophones, Francophones or CamFranAnglophones.* Instead of helping Cameroonians to fulfil the three following duties as described by Tiomajou *"national integration, international communication and cooperation, acquisition of scientific and technical knowledge"[263]*, bilingualism divides them. Cameroonians are stuck and are blocking the living together for future generations with various dividing lines that Africans should be ashamed of. English and French are invaluable wealth for Cameroon, but turning them into social boundaries that divide *Us and You* is logically the negation of African culture, a waiver, a belittlement of Cameroon's *local* in the *global.*

Under a completely different perspective, it should also be noted that Anglophone Cameroonians from the North-West have very little in common with those of the South-West with regard to African languages, cultures and traditions that they practice. Anglophones of the South-West that is the Bakweri, the Bayangue, and the Bakossi are *Coastal Bantu* natives, therefore very close to the Sawa of the Littoral and the Ocean Division in the South. Similarities in names, languages, customs and traditions are obvious between the Anglophones of the South-West and Sawa in general. Anglophones of the North-West that is the Widikum, the Fulani, the Mogham, and the Nso are Tikar of Sudanese origin. They share the same meta-ethnic group

---

[261] This is the case with my colleagues Christopher Nhso, Devine Che Neba, Cage Banseka and many others.

[262] As several infant and primary schools, the Mfandena New Century Bilingual School of Yaoundé has a pedagogic approach that allows children to study all subject (mathematics, history, information, environmental science...) in both English and French. The Etoug-Ebe Bilingual High School offers a completely Bilingual BEPC.

[263] Tiomajou, David: op.cit. p.262

with the Bamileke and the Bamoun of the West. African languages spoken by Anglophones of the North-West such as the Mungaka, the Yamba, the Lamnso, the Ngemba has the same sound system as well as the same semantics with sister languages of the Bamileke of the West. The same customs and traditions, the same fabrics and traditional clothing design are found with the Anglophones of the North-West as well as the Francophone Bamileke of the West.[264] In Cameroon, two politicized ethnic constructions bring out millennium affinities between the Anglophones of the South-West and the Sawa and between the Anglophones of the North-West and the Bamileke. These are the *"Grand Sawa Movement"*[265] which in 1996 brought together all the Sawa elites from the Atlantic Coast starting from Mamfe to Campo to denounce the political dominance of Bamileke immigrants within the CPDM and the SDF in Douala. For its supporters, this Pan-Sawa movement was the sole means of protection against the dominance of the West and North-West immigrants: (the Anglo-Bamileke) not only in the littoral but also in the South-West. The second construction is the *"Anglo-Bamileke"*[266] concept or *Anglo-Bami*. The Anglo-Bami concept thus refers to the Anglophone Cameroonians of the North-West and their Bamileke cultural neighbors and brothers of the West who during the democratic transition of the 1990s were accused of having formed an alliance within the Social Democratic Front (SDF) with the intention of overthrowing president Paul Biya's regime in order to take the political power in Yaoundé. This means that the alliance between North-West Anglophones and those of the South-West of Cameroon only last as long as

---

[264] A personal experience is worth mentioning here to illustrate the thesis of cultural ties between the Bamileke Cameroonians and the Anglophone Cameroonians of the North-West: I am a Bamileke Francophone from Mbouda in the West and my colleague, Banseka Cajetan Lukong is Anglophone from Kumbo in the North-West. We often pay regular visits to our parents in both regions almost every year from the past 10 years. We were struck by the linguistic similarities and cultural rites between the two villages right from the first visits in 2007. When Banseka's mother, Mrs Anasthasia Lukong talks to me in Lamnso, I am not totally lost and it is the same when my mother, Mrs Cecile Keongne talks to Banseka in Ngomba, he is not a complete foreigner.

[265] Nyamnjoh, Francis/Rowlands, Michael: op.cit.p.331–332

[266] Verdier, Isabelle: Cameroun 100 hommes de pouvoirs 1. Edition Indingo Publication Paris-France, 1997 p.29or Mbock, Charly: op.cit. p.53

they can politically exploit it for separatist and secessionist ends, colonial linguistic legacy that is the British language and culture inherited from the Trusteeship period. As a matter of fact, the cohabitation history between the populations of both regions is marked by several episodes of expression of violence and frustration of the South-West populations towards North-West immigrants who have come to the South-West to work in large banana, rubber, pineapple, coffee plantations and others. These North-West immigrants are stigmatized by the natives of the South-West depending on the socio-political constellation for instance *"cam no go"*[267] and today the language has changed and it is *"cam we rest"*. *Cam we rest* and fight together against the exterior enemy. The Anglophones of the North-West, very often with the Bamileke are perceived as invaders (*Cam no go*) when they have to share resources. But when they have to discuss the Anglophone problem with regard to Francophone marginalization, the links are strengthened between the Anglophones of the North-West and those of the South-West and *"cam no go"* refers thus to all Francophones of all ethnic groups. At this moment, Francophones especially the Bamileke, born, bred and educated in the South-West and the North-West are stigmatized as Francophones and are not part of *Cam we rest*. The alliances between both groups thus vary depending on the nature of the political stakes and actors in competition.

If the English-speaking world as an identity reference in Cameroon operates at a variable geopolitical degree, it is however, not realistic to conclude that there is no *Anglophone Problem or Question* in Cameroon. Still another fantasy for some and for others, a political bubble, confined in the political literature some time ago, the *Anglo-*

---

[267] *"Cam no go"* is a phrase in Pidgin English referring to an endemic skin disease which is very rampant in the South-West region with the specificity that once infected, one can never get rid of it as it becomes drug resistant. Refer to: Arrey, William Hermann: Divided Societies and ethno-regional antagonism: « A study of the social interaction between Anglophone North Westerners and South Westerners in Bua, South West Cameroon », Master's Degree Thesis in Peace and Conflict Transformation, Center for Peace Studies, University of Tromso, Norway, 2004–2006, pp.4, 21,38,40,55. *"Cam no go"* also applies to Francophones that have made a lot of money in both Anglophone regions of Cameroon.

*phone problem* has taken a very worrying turn since November, 21st 2016, starting with teachers' and lawyers' protests against the *francophonization* of the Anglophone education and justice systems, in a few months, they have moved to federalist protests for the moderates and secessionist protests for the hardliners.[268] Today it is clear that it is *"the Anglophone case…which has lasted for a long time…"* and not *"a lawyers' or teachers' problem."*[269] One may wonder why after 42 years of separation and 56 years of reunification and unity, Cameroonians are where they are today: re-calling into question the national living together? How have Cameroonians got to such *retro celebration of enslavement* and of *the myth of a happy colonization?* to rightly quote Achille Mbembe.[270]

Attempts to answer this question can be formulated at two levels. There is the turbulent process of decolonization and its political legacy associated to the question of governance in independent Cameroon. In fact, the decolonization process of Cameroon has resulted in what some researchers and historians have described in terms of *stolen independence* because it was *artificial* or *negotiated* in the spirit of *Francafrique* sophistication and implementation. That is the implementation of *"this specific neocolonial system of governance that allows a small number of French officials in collusion with a handful of African leaders to control from a distance and at a reasonable price what…Charles Lacheroy will describe as tadpole states: states with a fat head…under developed people prisoners of a system that maintains them under the dominance of the former Metropole…"*[271] Cameroon definitely signed bilateral cooperation agreements with France on November 13th 1960. These are agreements and conven-

---

268 The position of the Madrid government supported by the EU in the Catalan crisis in Spain in 2017 reinforces the official stand of the Cameroonian government which is for a "one and indivisible nation".

269 Nsoh, Christopher & Dzé-Nwa, Willibroad in *Le Jour* N°2534, Jeudi 05 Octobre 2017, p.2–3

270 Mbembé, Achille in http://www.lemonde.fr/afrique/article/2017/10/09/au-cameroun-le-crepuscule-d-une-dictature-a-huis-clos_5198501_3212.html, consulté le 10/10/2017 à 11:46

271 Deltombe, Thomas &al.: op.cit. pp.137–195

tions that *strictly control Cameroon sovereignty in the military, economic, monetary, diplomatic, cultural sectors…the neocolonial heritage that permanently links Cameroon to France is signed in almost complete silence.*[272] In the Federal Republic (1961) and the United Republic of Cameroon (1972), these Francafrique based texts together with the Jacobin highly centralized state system were applied to the Anglophone regions,[273] with a population that have been governed by the *Indirect Rule,* that is, with a true margin of maneuver in the management of public affairs. Anglophones' feeling of being purely annexed, reached a critical point in 1984 where the name United Republic simply became the Republic of Cameroon, thus erasing all traces of a few decades of history of the country's name as well as the reduction of the number of stars on the national flag.

The second answer is found in the feeling of socio-political and economic marginalization that Cameroonian Anglophones rightly or wrongly have with regard to the governance of the country. They feel that they are breached in the republic with regard to infrastructures and the sharing of resources while their soil, especially in the South-West has most of the oil that Cameroon has exported since 1970 and large agricultural production is also on their land. It is along this line that Eyoh Dickson states *"The marginalisation of Anglophones…is the result of a process of nation-state building that has been defined by the determination of the francophone elite to erase the cultural and institutional bases of former West Cameroon's distinctiveness…The emergence of oil, which is wholly derived from South West Province, as the primary source of state income…reinforce these claims as the new oil wealth was seen to feed spectacular levels of*

---

[272] Ibid.: p.186

[273] It must be noted that agreements and conventions signed at the end of 1958 about among other things the exclusivity reserved to France about the exploitation of the sub-soil resources, were signed between two legally unequal partners: France and Cameroon under the trusteeship. Their final ratification took place before the October 1961 reunification. In the light of this, it could be easier to establish a comparison between the June 2016 British exit (Brexit) in Europe and the dangerous awakening of the November 2016 Anglophone secessionist movement in Cameroon.

*official corruption and patronage at the expense of Anglophone"*[274]
To this is added the fact that *feeling discriminated, Anglophones complain that they have never had most prestigious positions of the country. They have neither had the Executive Secretary of the presidency nor key ministries such as the Defence, Territorial Administration, External Relations and Economy...*[275] The double feeling of annexation and marginalization has, hence, led the Anglophone to a double feeling of discrimination and frustration. As an extra-African identity element, the English-speaking world is today exploited by the followers and the hawks of Cameroon secession by all means. Contrary to Akere Muna's reluctance[276] between the fact that either Anglophone would have a problem or they could be a problem in Cameroon, the Anglophone problem may be understood as a socio-political statement of dissatisfaction or the rejection of the Anglophone regarding the central power of Yaoundé with the political process of institutional and cultural assimilation; and also their discrimination with regard to the sharing of political and administrative resources and finally wronging their regions in infrastructural development. Aware of the potential threat of Anglophones, there have been statesmen such as John Ngu Foncha, Salomon Tandeng Muna, Achidi Achu, Philemon Yang, Chief Emmanuel Mbela Lifafa Endeley, Peter Mafani Musonge, Inoni Ephraim, Atanga Nji who have been and still are great senior civil servants in the Cameroonian state of both regimes. The participation of some Anglophone elite in very high administrative levels in Ahidjo's and Biya's regimes have not changed Anglophones' feeling of discrimination and frustration that have become a major concern for the territorial integrity and sovereignty of Cameroon since November 2016.

In this constellation of **7+1 Strategic and Conflicting Groups** which, in addition to ethno-regional diversity and identities (meso-conflicts),

---

[274] Eyoh, Dickson: op.cit. P.247. In the current crisis, an Anglophone (Mr. Atanga Nji Paul) was appointed ministry of territorial administration in 2018.

[275] Dougueli, Goerges: op.cit. p.36

[276] Muna, Akere: Le Monde s'effondre...in: http://www.foretiafoundation.org/wp-content/uploads/2017/07/Akere-Muna_THINGS-FALL-APART-min.pdf, consulté le 13/09/2017, p.3

there is now an element of civilizational division (mega-conflict), the balance of Cameroon is on a quicksand. Only Cameroonians can consolidate this foundation or topple it. Therefore, awakening the war demon or adopting a posture of intolerance is not worthy of the intelligence of Cameroonians. One must visit a country in war or undergoing post-conflict reconstruction to understand the very special gift that Cameroon has: Peace even if it is Negative. When the war demon wakes up, nobody knows when and how it will stop, neither the number of casualties that it will make, nor the amount of breakage or irreversible social animosity it will leave behind. Since 2006, I have proposed the model of **Democratic Rotation in High Office Position** to the political analysis and political debates, hoping that this can be a political stopgap measure to transcend and transform diversity, ethnoregional identities and civilizational division inherited from the turbulent colonial past of Cameroon.

### *Electoral Regions in Cameroon*

We have successfully demonstrated the inconsistency of the colonial anthropology and ethnology in their excessive business of fragmentation of the ethnic landscape of the country into more or less than 200 groups. From the two constructivists' and essentialists' perspectives, we indicated **7+1** ethnic meta-groups in Cameroon, which are: The Pahouin, the Fulani, the Bamileke, the Sawa, the Bassa, the Bamoun, the Kirdi and the Anglophones. In order to introduce Democratic Rotation in the Head of State Position to Cameroon, it would be important to undertake a territorial division of the country into **Electoral Regions** which beyond the current administrative regions take into account the ethnographic structure of Cameroon and the dots and links that exist between the 7+1 identified groups. The study that we carried out in 2006 and 2012, in this respect, might still be worthy of interest. We have updated it in the current context and come out with the following **four (4) large Electoral Regions** that more or less constitute the geographical reference of the 7+1 strategic and conflicting groups:

**The Coastal Region** (the Francophone Sawa, the Anglophone Sawa of the South-West, the Bassa of the Littoral…)

**The Equator Region** (the Pahouin, the Bassa of the Center, the Mbam people…)

**The Grassland Region** (the Bamileke, the Anglophones of the North-West and the Bamoun)

**The Sahel Region** (the Fulani, the Haoussa, the Kanuri and the Kirdi...)

The current (10) administrative regions will remain the same for administrative proximity and subsidiarity through an effective decentralization. In the case of a return to federalism, those (4) Electoral Regions could well become Federal States. Cameroonians will avoid the danger of the leadership falling apart following a two state federalism by introducing Rotation in the High Office between four (4) large Electoral Regions. Following is the geographical representation of these four Electoral Regions or Federal States.

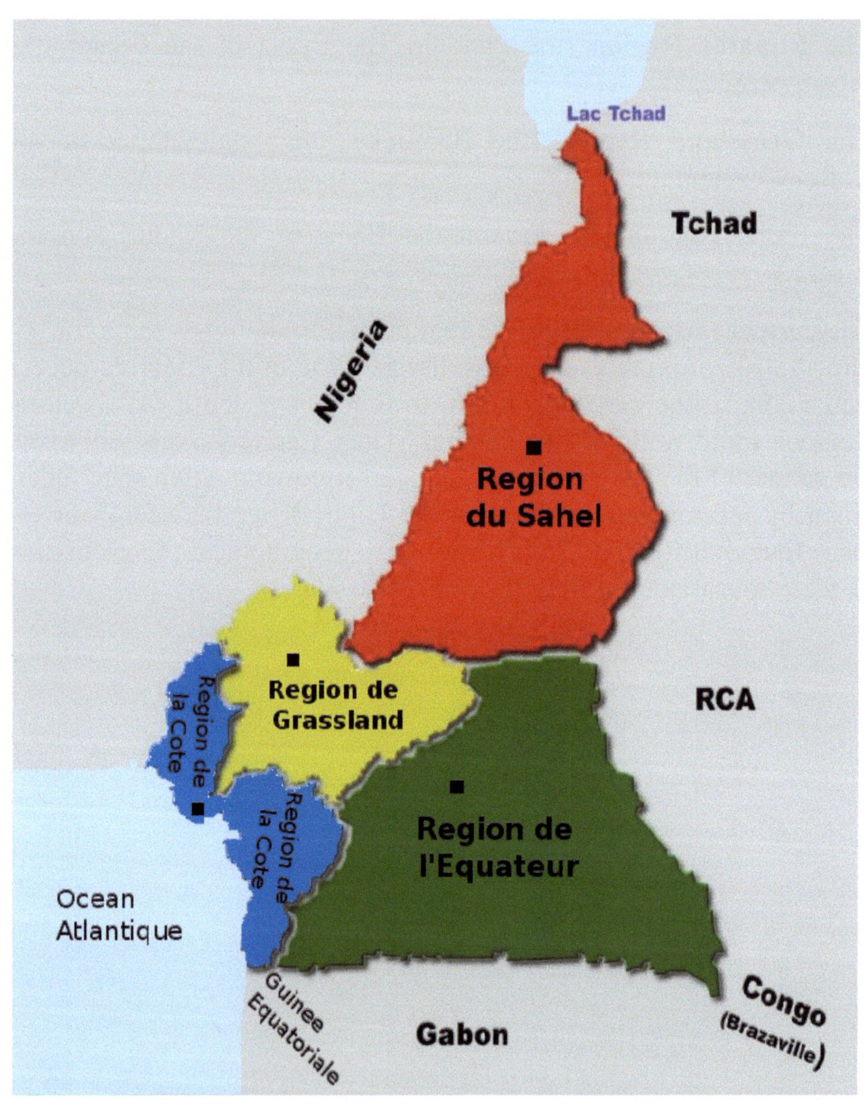


*Source: Tagou (2006) up-dated*

### *Rotation Cycle in Cameroon*

As it has been demonstrated several times, here and elsewhere, the sharing of power and resources through regional balance policy established by the Ahidjo's regime and maintained by Biya's, has provided Cameroon with political stability until the outbreak of the *Boko*

154

*Haram* phenomenon and the resurgence of the *Anglophone problem.* Under both regimes, ethno-regional criteria have always guided the appointment of Ministers and members of the various governments of the republic, and Managers in public administration and in large parastatal companies. Most recently, the elections and appointment of senators followed the same ethno-regional representation. With only a few exceptions,[277] the elections of council advisors, mayors, members of parliament follow the same principle of native candidates which bring out the 7+1 groups that we have identified. The policy of regional balance with regard to the sharing of powers and resources would not and has never been applied to the highest and the most powerful position, the presidency of the Republic. The presidential seat would not be divided and shared like a cake. The Democratic Rotation in High Office supplements this physical and socio-political inconvenience. With the implementation of Democratic Rotation at this top level of political power, the High Office of the Republic will rotate between the four large **Electoral Regions** at the rhythm of two presidential terms of 5 years per Electoral Region.[278]

In addition, political realism will compel Cameroonians to start the Rotation cycle with the Equator Region in order to appease the fear of the Pahouin ethnic group and reassure them that Democratic Rotation in Office is not a political trick to push them out of their Strategic Group position. But much more a democracy model that will in the long run allow all groups, small ones and large ones to feel that they are full-fledged citizens of Cameroon; that is deeply accepted by others and with equal opportunities to participate in elections. The first Rotation cycle in Cameroon will be as follows:

---

[277] These exceptions are cases of Bamileke elected parliamentarians and mayors out of their region of origin, the West. They are Mr. Paul Eric Djomgoué, CPDM parliamentarian in the Nfoundi Division (Yaoundé II) and late Mrs. Foning Françoise (Mayor in Douala V), Mr. Dagobert Fampou, Mr. Tchato Abraham and Mrs. Dénise Fampou (successively Mayor in Douala II).

[278] Contrary to my initial proposal in 2006, a seven year term will make the cycle longer, therefore the need to return to the five years term.

**1st Round 2018 – 2028:** *The President is from the Equatorial Region* therefore from the Pahouin ethnic group or Bassa of Nyong-et-Kéllé

**2nd Round 2028 – 2038:** *The President is from the Coastal Region,* therefore Francophone Sawa or Anglophone Sawa from the South-West or Bassa from Sanaga Maritime…

**3rd Round 2038 – 2048:** *The President is from the Grassland Region* therefore Bamiléké, Anglophone from the North-West or Bamoun

**4th Round 2048 – 2058:** *The President is from the Sahel Region* therefore Fulani, Haoussa, Kanuri or Kirdi

This means that in 2018,[279] all political parties in Cameroon wishing to take part in presidential elections will nominate a candidate from the Equatorial Region for the universal suffrage of all Cameroonian citizens. For example Bello Bouba would not be the natural **UNDP** candidate, but a citizen, native of the Equatorial Electoral Region whom Bello Bouba will campaign for in all the Sahel Region. The same will apply to the **SDF**, Chairman **John Fru Ndi and Josua Oshi** will mobilise Anglophones of the North and South-West to vote for a certain Atangana, Mballa, Ndongo, Mbarga,Mbassi, Matip, Bock, Bidias, Dumbe, Eboa, Mafani, Musonge,Ngole Ngole… as SDF candidate for presidential elections of the 1st and 2nd Rounds of the Rotation. That would be the case until the 3rd and 4th rounds when **Paul Biya** will go to Mvomeka and **Mama Fouda** to Yaoundé on a campaign trail for a certain Djomgoue, Muna, Kamga,

---

[279] The candidacy of Barrister Akere Muna (PFD), Njifor Afanwi Francklin (MCNC) and Osih Joshua (SDF) would discard a potential boycott of the 2018 presidential elections in both Anglophone regions. A boycott could have invaluable political and institutional consequences on the legitimacy of the ballot per se and especially on the political stability of Cameroon in next months. Their candidacy and that of Professor Maurice Kamto are disturbing elements in the Rotation cycle that has been put forward for 2018 in Cameroon. We hope that the main political actors would wisely transcend their personal ambitions for the interest of peace and stability in Cameroon in 2018 and agree on a cycle of rotation that meets the current context and that would contribute to the resolution of the Anglophone Problem and there preserve the territorial integrity of Cameroon and booster national reconciliation in the country.

Tchinda,Yemga, Ayafor, Fai,…or Bouba, Ousman, Ahatou, Gwoda, Alawadi…because they are CPDM (Cameroon People Democratic Movement) candidates respectively in the Grassland and Sahel Electoral Regions etc.

But if there is here and there, a leap forward to the resolution of the Anglophone problem by transcending and transforming it positively, and to national reconciliation, with safeguards for the political witch hunt, Cameroon can return to my 2006 proposals and begin the rotation either with the **Atlantic Coast Region** or with the **Grassland Region**. The other two regions namely the **Sahel Region** and the **Equator Region** will follow one after another for they have already been at the central power. Current political elite of the government or the opposition would have demonstrated positive transcendence and transformation of micro-conflicts that Cameroon has been facing since independence and accurately today with the Anglophone problem. If the rotation has to begin either with Atlantic Coast Region or the Grassland one, this will give an Anglophone Cameroonian a chance to become the Head of State. The upcoming presidential elections constitute a high risk political event for Cameroon, if they take place, as scheduled on the 7th October 2018, without a total resolution of the Anglophone crisis and restauration of peace in Cameroon.

This new political practice will establish a good predisposition and give a positive wake-up call in the socio-political psychology of current Cameroonians. It would pave the way for the permanent transcendence and transformation of ethno-regional conflicts into a new situation in which all Cameroonians of the future will live in peace because they would mutually accept each other, because they would have equal opportunities to take part in the management of public affairs from the lowest level to the highest office of the Republic, that is the Presidency of the Republic. This practice, this new democratic scenario will alleviate the fear of those who are afraid of losing the power for good with the demographic law and appease the frustration of those who will no longer be considered as different Cameroonians, condemned to remain in the periphery of the supreme power. Ethno-regional diversity will then become flowers to embellish the cultural garden of *Africa in miniature*. The English-Speaking World and the French-Speaking World will no longer be dividing lines between *Us and You*, but exterior assets for every Positive Peace-loving Cameroonian who does not only want to conquer the globalizing world but also and above all to bring a civilizational input to humanity.

Democratic Rotation in High Office, coupled with an effective administrative decentralization according to the 1996 constitution or to a four (4) states Federalism[280] and to the sharing of other resources on the basis of a dosage between regional balance and meritocracy, thus stands as a solution *to all the crisis, the questions and all the problems* of Cameroonians with regard to political acceptance and participation as well as to the re-distribution of resources. It is a solution to *this mistrust* which causes problems[281] between Cameroonians with regard to their ethnic origins. All problems, all crises and other questions between Cameroonians that divide people today will be undermined in their destabilizing and separatist contents. [282] *Cameroon does not need either a Francophone State or an Anglophone one, but a decolonized, multicultural, multilingual and democratic Pan African State.*[283] Democratic Rotation in High Office stands as a political and institutional approach that can help Cameroonians to build that republican State. Over 80 years of rotation, Cameroonians would have had two rounds of rotation, a new generation of Cameroonians used to political change at the Head of the State position, completely

---

[280] If, in the extreme case, we must return to federalism, it should be a four state federalism and not two, operating like in the GFR with its micro-economic *Ausgleichssystem* between the federate states. This is economic equalization that exists between federate states in the GFR, where under the control of the federal government, strong economic states help the weak states. Even though Bavaria, which had long benefited from it wanted at some point to put this principle into question.

[281] Dougueli, Georges: op.cit.p.39

[282] During a full round of Democratic Rotation, an Anglophone Cameroonian will have two (2) opportunities over four (4) to become the Head of State of Cameroon. Meanwhile the others Groups will have only one opportunity over four.

[283] Mbembe, Achille in: http://www.lemonde.fr/afrique/article/2017/10/09/au-cameroun-le-crepuscule-d-une-dictature-a-huis-clos_5198501_3212.html consulted on 10/10/2017 at 11:46

self-confident and reconciled with their true history, will emerge. That generation of Cameroonians may decide to come back to liberal democracy or to carry on with Democratic Rotation in High Office. What is most important is that they would be able to say that *they are proud of being native of the same country with Ruben Um Nyobe, Mongo Beti, Jean-Marc Ela, Eboussi Boulaga, John Ngu Foncha, Manu Dibango, Roger Milla or Achille Mbembe...*[284] and including Ernest Ouandie, Felix Moumie, Ahmadou Ahidjo, Tandeng Muna, Achidi Achu, Philemon Yang, Victor Mukete, Peter Mafany Musonge, Marcel Niat Njifendji, Paul Biya etc.

---

[284] Essomba, Armand Leka: « Qu'est-ce qu'être Camerounais ? in *Jeune Afrique* N°2963–2964 du 22 Octobre au 4 Novembre 2017, p.36

# CONCLUSION

If Cameroonians want to use the same words, the same concepts to mean the same thing in the 21$^{st}$ century, then the concepts *Ethnic Group, People, Nation* and *State* must be dusted off from their European 17$^{th}$ and 19$^{th}$ centuries' connotations. The new democratic scenario brings challenges not only to African countries but also to old democracies. Here, it is noticed that *a policy of enmity, ("politique d'inimitié"),* is being implemented in a *society of enmity, ("société d'inimitié"),* which, in turn, is fully *going out of democracy ("sortie de la démocratie").*[285] African countries are getting into democracy and the question is: which model should be implemented? Beyond integrative and consociational models coupled with power sharing advocated in the literature, the choice has been made about the Jacobin liberal model which, unfortunately raises more problems in divided societies. Alternative models have been put forward. But their weaknesses are in their naïve optimism reversed from ancestral and pre-colonial systems whose efficiency had hardly been proved yesterday and before and whose applicability is today impossible in Republics time.

Based on its beneficial results in the supranational large gatherings' governance and minimally in some countries and socio-political and religious associations, the rotation principle has been associated to the democratic mode of access to supreme power, as a solution to conflicts related to ethno-regional diversity in a given country. We provided a simulation of this model with Ivory Coast and Cameroon cases; two countries with clearly known diversity. At the same time, this model is either a chance and opportunity or a potential threat. Its *transferability* will require not only contextual case studies in other countries suffering from an irreversible and exploited diversity as in the current case of Kenya[286], but also supplementary analysis on oth-

---

[285] Mbembe, Achille: op.cit. (2016)

[286] In Kenya, Rotation Democracy is a solution between the big ethnic groups, Kikuyu, Luhya, Kalenjin, Luo, who are at the heart of the current electoral crisis. A rotation between these groups would alleviate current political tensions between supporters of the

er aspects such as the implementation of rotation in regions or federal state and on the deep causes of the various obstacles to electoral processes known here and there on the continent since 1990. If democracy is the least bad of political systems, Democratic Rotation in High Office stands as the lesser democratic evil in divided societies where national consciousness, political culture and citizenship are not fully developed and established.

We would like to bring this little thought to conclusion by opening the debate with our remarks of 2011 at a conference in Trinity College, Washington, D.C.: *"Stagnation is not a warranty for sustainable stability. Even in the cosmos nothing is fixed and stagnant, all planets in the solar system are constantly gravitating or rotating around the sun and that is what makes the equilibrium of the whole system. I believe that this model is worth further discussion, research on its adaptation on other countries with strong diversities and a try"*[287] While waiting for the political spirit of the time to evolve to test the Democratic Rotation in High Office, the urgency of the matter, is there for all the radical minds here and elsewhere, of today and the future which denounce marginalization on every platform and that allegedly defend ethno-regional, religious and radical interests in exclusive aggressiveness between *Us and You*.

The model of Democratic Rotation in High Office ought to be comprehended as political asset to Johan Galtung's meso and mega-conflict transcendence and transformation approach at the level of a nation.

---

outgoing president, **Uhuru Kenyatta** (Kikuyu) and his challenger **Raila Amoto Odinga** (Luo) and would save Kenya from a Somalia type of destabilization. We hope the reconciliation process promised by the two leaders in Mai 2019 will lead to a durable transcendence and transformation of ethnic rivalries Kenya.

[287] Tagou, Célestin: op.cit. (2013): p.159

# BIBLIOGRAPHY


**Agbu, Osita A.:** Ethnicity and Democratisation in Africa, Challenges for politics and development. Discussion Paper62. Nordiska Afrikainstitutet, Uppsala, 2011

**Ahidjo, Ahmadou:** Contribution à la construction nationale. Présence Africaine, Paris, 1964

**Allen, Goerge &al.:** The consequences of Negociated Settlements in Civil Wars 1945–1993, American Political Science Review 89

**Alter, Peter (ed.):** Nationalismus. Dokumente zur Geschichte und Gegenwart eines Phänomens. München 1994

**Anderson, Benedict:** Die Erfindung der Nation. Zur Karriere eines folgenreichen Konzepts, Frankfurt/M 1988

**Assefa, Gidey:** Ethnonationale Konflikte, Föderalismus und Demokratie in Äthiopien. Online Veröffentlichung, Frankfurt am Main 2002

**Bahoken, J.C. & Atangana, Engelbert:** Cultural policy in the united republic of Cameron. The Unesco Press. Paris 1976

**Balibar, Etienne:** Is there a Neo-Racism, in: Balibar/Wallerstein (Hg): Race, Nation, Class. Ambiguos Indentites, London New York 1991

**Banseka, Cage:** The Anglophone Problem in Cameroon: A Conflict Resolution Perspective in: African Renaissance Vol. 3 No.2 March/April 2006

**Barth, Fredrik:** Ethnic Groups and Boundaries: The social organization of culture Difference; Oslo/Bergen/Tromso, 1969

**Bayart, Jean François:** La problématique de la démocratie en Afrique noire « La Baule, et puis après ? » in: Politique Africaine N° 43, Octobre 1991

**Bercovitch, Jacob & al:** Regional guide to international conflict and management from 1945 to 2003, Congressional Quarterly, 2004

**Berman, Bruce:** Ethnicity, Patronage and the african state: The politics of uncivil nationalism in: African Affairs vol. 97

**Berry, Brewton:** Race Relations: The Interaction of Ethnic and Racial Groups, Boston: Houghton Mifflin.1951

**Betche Zachée:** Le Phénomène Boko Haram au-délà du radicalisme. L'Harmattan 2016

**Biya, Paul:** Pour le Libéralisme Communautaire, Éditions Marcel Fabre, Lausanne, 1987

**Black, Duncan:** On the Rationale of Group Decision-making in: Journal of Political Economy, 56(1) (1948): pp.23–34.

**Breitinger, Eckhard:** Defining News Idioms and Alternative Forms of Expression, Cross/ Culter, 23, Amsterdam-Atlanta 1996

**Brunner/Conze/Koselleck (Hg.):** Geschichtliche Grundbegriffe, Bd. 7, 1992

**Césaire, Aimé:** Discours sur le colonialisme, suivi du Discours sur la Négritude, Présence Africaine, 2004

**Chanteur, Janine (1989):** La paix un défi contemporain, L'Harmattan, 1994

**Chapman, Malcon &al.:** Introduction. History and Social Anthropology, 1989

**Cohen, Ronald:** Ethnicity: problem and Focus in Anthropology, in: Annual review of Anthropology, Vol. 7, 1978

**Czempiel, E.O.:** Friedensstrategien. Systemwandel durch Internationale Organisationen, Demokratisierung und Wirtschaft. Paderborn 1986.

**David Birmingham/Phyllis M. Martin** (Hrsg.): History of Central Africa. The contemporary years since 1960, London/New York 1998

**Deltombe, Thomas & al.:** La guerre du Cameroun: l'invention de la Françafrique, La Découverte, Paris 2016

**Deutsch, Karl W.:** Nationenbildung – Nationalstaat – Integration. Westdeutscher Verlag, Wiesbaden,1972

**Deutsches Kolonialblatt** XVI, 1905

**Ditrich, Eckhard J.:** Das Weltbild des Rassismus, Frankfurt, Cooperative Verlag 1991

**Dittrich, Eckard J. / Radtke, Frank-Olaf**(Hg.): Ethnizität Wissenschaft und Minderheiten, Opladen: Westdeutscher Verlag. 1990

**Dongmo, Jean-Louis:** Le Dynamisme Bamiléké (Cameroun), Yaoundé 1981

**Eriksen, Thomas Hylland:** Ethnicity and Nationalism. Athropogical Perspectives, London: Pluto 1993

**Erny, Pierre:** Rwanda 1994 Clés pour comprendre le calvaire d'un peuple. L'Harmattan 1994

**Estel, Bernd:** Das Prinzip Nation in modernen Gesellschaften. Länderdiagnosen und historische Perspektiven, Westdeutacher Verlag 1994

**Ferdinand De Saussure:** *Écrits de linguistique générale* (éd. par Simon Bouquet; Rudolf Engler, Antoinette Weil), Paris: Gallimard, 2002

**Finkelstein, Norman G.:** The Holocaust Industry: Reflections on the Exploitation of Jewish Suffering. ISBN-13: 978-1859843239, 2000

**Fluer-Lobban &al.:** Tribes: A Socio-political Analysis, in: Ufahamu, vol.7, No.1 1976

**Galtung, Johan:** Transcendance et Transformation des Conflits: une introduction au métier de médiateur. Traduction française de **Célestin Tagou**, PUPA, 2010, Yaoundé

**Ibid.:** A theory of Peace: Building Direct, Structural and Cultural and Peace, Kolon Press, 20120

**Gellner, Ernest**: Nations and Nationalism, Oxford. Blackwell 1983

**Giddens, A:** Emile Durkheim Selected Writings, Cambridge University Press, 1972a

**Ibd.:** Capitalism and Modern Social Theory, Cambridge University Press, 1971

**Gordon M:** Human nature, class and ethnicity, New York, Oxford University Press, 1978

**Glazer, N. D.P., Moyniham**(eds), Ethnicity, Theory and Experience, Cambrige, Mass, Harvard University Press, 1975

**Gramizzi, Claudio:** « La crise ivoirienne de la tentative de coup d'état au gouvernement de réconciliation nationale »: Rapport du Groupe de recherche et d'information sur la paix et la sécurité (GRIP) Bruxelles

**Guenther, Roth &al**.: Weber Max, Economy and Society, Bedminster Press, New York, 1968

**Gwoda, Adder & al.** (sd.): Le Nord-Cameroun à l'épreuve des pluralismes, L'Harmattan, Paris, 2012

**H.M. kallen** (ed.): Culture and Democraty in the United States, New York, Boni and Liveright, 1924

**Habermas, Jürgen**: Der DM-Nationalismus in: Die Zeit, 30. März 1990, n° 14

**Heckmann, Friedrich**: Ethnische Minderheiten, Volk und Nation, Stuttgart, Enke Verlag. 1992

**Horowitz, Donald L**: Ethnic Groups in Conflict. University of California Press, Berkeley, 1985

**Hurd, D.**: Promoting Good Government. Crossbow, Autumn, 1990

**Joseph, Richard**: Le mouvement nationaliste au Cameroun. Ed. Karthala, 1986

**Kamto, Maurice (sd.)**: L'Afrique dans un monde en mutation. Dynamiques internes, marginalisation internationale ? Paris, Afrédit, 2010

**Kant, Emmanuel**: Kleinere Schriften zur Ethik und Religionsphilosophie, 1870

**Kayser, Christian&al**: in: Working for Sustainable Peace in Cameroon. CPS/EED, Bafoussam, Berlin 2011

**Konings, Piet/Nyamnjoh, Francis B.**: The Anglophone Problem in Cameroon, in: Journal of Modern African Studies, 35 (1997) 2

**Kum'a Ndumbé III.**: Was will Bonn in Afrika? Zur Afrikapolitik der Bundesrepublik Deutschland. Pfaffenweiler: Centaurus-Verl.-Ges.,1992

**Le Vine, Victor T.**: The Cameroon Federal Republic, Cornelle University Press, London, 1971

**Lentz, Astrid**: Ethnizität und Macht. Ethnische Differenzierung als Struktur und Prozeß sozialer Schließung im Kapitalismus, Köln: Papy Rossa. 1995

**Lentz, Carola**: Die Konstruktion von Ethnizität. Eine politische Geschichte Nord-West Ghanas, 1870–1990 Rüddiger Köppe Verlag; Köln 1998

**Ibid.**: "Tribalismus" und Ethnizität in Afrika: eine Forschungsüberblick, das Arabische Buch, Berlin 1994

**Lewis, W. Arthur**: Politics in West Africa, London 1965

**Lijphart, Arend:** Democracy in Plural Societies: A Comparative Exploration. Yale University Press, new Haven, 1977

**Ibid.:** Power Sharing in South Africa: Policy papers in International Affairs. University of California Press, Berkeley, 1985

**Ibid.:** The politics of Accommodation: Pluralism and Democracy in the Netherlands. University of California Press, Berkeley, 1968;

**Little, Kenneth:** Color and Commonsenes: Fabian Society and Commwealth Bureau 1958

**Lukes, S.:** Emile Durkheim, London, Macmillan, 1973

**Lutz-Bachmann, Mathias &al**(ed.): Weltstaat oder Staatenwelt? Frankfurt am Main, 2002

**Mbembe, Achille**: Critique de la raison nègre, Editions La Découverte, Paris, 2013

**Ibid.:** Politique de l'inimitié, Editions La Découverte, Paris 2016

**Mbock, Charly Gabriel** (sd).: Les conflits ethniques au Cameroun: Quelles sources, quelles solutions ? Sep et Saagraph, Yaoundé, 2000

**Mbonimpa, Melchor:** Ethnicité et Démocratie en Afrique, l'homme tribal contre l'homme citoyen ? L'hamattan 1994

**Mbuyinga, Elenga:** Tribalisme et problème national en Afrique Noire. Le cas du Kamerun, L'Harmattan 1989

**Mehler, Andreas:** Kamerun in der Ära Biya: Bedingungen, erste Schritte und Blockaden einer demokratischen Transition. IAK, Hamburg, 1993

**Menthong, Helène-Laure:** Vote et communautarisme au Cameroun: un vote de cœur, de sang et de raison, in: Politique Africaine (1998) 69

**Mhone, Guy C.Z.:** Les défis de la gouvernance, de la réforme du secteur public et de l'administration publique en Afrique, University of Witwatersrand, Février 2003

**Mono Ndjana, Hubert:** L'idée sociale chez Paul Biya, Yaoundé, 1985

**Montville, Joseph V.(ed.).:** Conflict and Peacemaking in Multiethnic Societies, Lexington Books, New York, 1991

**Mühlmann, Wihelm E:** Rassen Ethnien, Kulturen. Moderne Ethnologie, Neuwied: Luchterland 1964

**Mveng, Engelbert:** Histoire du Cameroun. CEPER, Yaoundé 1984

**Ibid.:** Histoire du Cameroun. Paris 1963

**Njoya, Jean:** Démocratisation, divergences ethniques et politisation de la pluralité au Cameroun in: Canadian Journal of African Studies, 36 (2002) 2

**Nordlinger, Eric:** Conflict Regulation in Divided Societies, Center for International Affairs, Harvard University, 1972

**Nuhn, Walter:** Kamerun unter dem Kaiseradler, Neue überarbeitete Auflage, Juni 2000

**Nyambjoh, Francis/Rowlands, Mechale:** Elite Associations and the politics of Belonging in Cameroun, in: African Affairs, (1998) 68,3

**Nyamnjoh, Francis:** Cameroon: A country united by ethnic ambition and difference, in: African Affairs, (1999)

**Obenga, Théophile:** Cheikh Anta Diop, volney et le Sphnix. Présence Africaine, 1996

**Ibid.:** Les Bantu Langues-Peuples-Civilisations. Présence Africaine, 1985

**Owona, Joseph:** Les Systèmes politiques précoloniaux, Paris, L'Harmattan 2015

**Pondi, Jean-Emmanuel** (ed.): Repenser le développement à partir de l'Afrique, Afredit, Yaoundé 2011

**Ibid.**: Thomas Sankara et l'Emergence de l'Afrique au 21°siècle, AfricEveil, Yaoundé 2015

**Poutignat, Philippe& al.**: Théories de l'éthnicité. Presses Universitaires de France, 1995

**Prélot, Marcel/Lescuyer Georges:** Histoire des idées politiques 13° Edition Dalloz 1997

**Preston, P.W:** Development Theory, an Introduction, Blackwell Publishing 2002

**Rapport de Human Rights Watch:** «La meilleure école: La violence estudiantine, l'impunité et la crise en Côte d'Ivoire », Human Rights Watch New York, 2005

**Razafindrakoto, Mireille & al:** Gouvernance et démocratie en Afrique: la population a son mot à dire in: Afrique Contemporaine, N°220, 2006

**Rex, John and Mason, David** (Hg.): Theories of Race and Ethnic Relations, Cambridge Cambridge University Press, 1986

**Rist, Gilbert:** Le développement Histoire d'une croyance occidentale, Presse de Science Po. 1996

**Rittberger, V.** (ed.): Theorien der Internationalen Beziehungen. Bestandaufnahme und Forschungsperspektiven (PVS Sonderheft 21), Opladen, (71–89)

**Rothchild, Donald &al**.(ed.): Sustainable Peace Power and Democracy after Civil Wars, Cornell University Press, Ithaca and London, 2005

**Rothchild, Donald:** Durable peace after Civil war: the structuring of ethnic interaction ULPA, Leipzig 2002

**Schlochauer, Hans-Jürgen:** Die Idee des ewigen Friedens, Ein Überblick über Entwicklung und Geltaltung des Friedenssicherungsgedankens auf der Grundlage einer Quellenauswahl, Ludwig Röhrscheid Verlag Bonn 1953

**Schmalz-Jacobsen & al.:** Ethnische Minderheiten in der Bundesrepublik Deutschland. Ein Lexikon, München. Beck 1995

**Schubert, Gunter & al:** Blockierte Demokratien in der Dritten Welt, Opladen 1998

**Sen, Amartya:** Development as Freedom, Oxford University Press, 1999

**Shils E.:** Primordial, personal, sacred and civil ties, British Journal of Sociology, 8, 1957

**Simo, David (sd):** Problématiques migratoires en contexte de globalisation, Les Grandes Editions, Yaoundé 2014 pp.159–184

**Sisk, Timothy D.:** Power Sharing and International Mediation in Ethnic conflicts, USIP Press, Washington, DC 2002

**Tadadjeu, Maurice:** Démocratie de Partage du Pouvoir; Pour le modèle P3 au Cameroun. Edition BUMA KOR, Yaoundé 1997

**Tagou, Célestin:** Demokratisches Rotationsprinzip, Cuvillier Verlag, Göttigen, 2006

**Ibid.: (ed.):** The dynamics of conflict, Peace and Development in African Societies, from local to international, Yaoundé, PUPA 2010

**Ibid.: (ed):** Gestion des Conflits en Afrique: Regards croisés de jeunes chercheurs de l'UPAc ; Revue Africaine de Paix, Communication et Développement, N°001-Nov2011, Yaoundé, PUPA 2011

**Ibid.:** Managing ethno-regional diversities in African states: Western peace paradigms versus African peace philosophy and a political way out in: Mapinduzi Journal vol.3, Berlin, 2013

**Ibid. (ed.):** Phénomène Boko Haram: Problématique de paix et sécurité au Cameroun face aux méga-conflits, Revue Africaine de Paix, Communication et Développement, Vol. 002, Yaounde, PUPA 2016

**Thompson, Richard H.:** Theories of Ethnicity. A critical Appraisal, New York: Greenwood Press,1989

**Van den Berghe P.L.:** Race and ethnicity: a sociobiological perspective in: Ethnic and Racial Studies, 1,4, 1978

**Verdier, Isabelle:** Cameroun 100 hommes de pouvoirs 1.Edition Indingo Publication Paris-France 1997

**Vincent J.:** The structuring of ethnicity in: Human organization, vol. 33, N° 4 1974, p. 375–378. Young C., The politics of cultural pluralism, Madison, University of Wisconsin Press, 1976

**Warnier, Jean Pierre:** « Archéologie et Histoire, Cameroun: le cas de l'Ouest », Communication présentée à la semaine de l'Histoire, Université de Yaoundé, avril 1981

**Ibid.:** L'Esprit d'entreprise au Cameroun, Paris, Karthala 1993

**Weber, Max:** Wirtschaft und Gesellschaft. Tübingen 1922

**Wiyghansaï Shaaghan Tumi, Christian:** Les deux Régimes Politiques d' Ahmadou Ahidjo. Macacos, 2006

**Yenshu Vebo, Emmanuel:** Levels of Historical Awarness. The Development of Identity and Ethnicity in Cameroon in: Cahiers d'Etudes africaines, 43 (2003)

**Jeune Afrique** N°2963–2964 du 22 octobre au 4 novembre 2017

**Le Jour** N°2534 du Jeudi 05 octobre 2017

http://wmedia.m.cameroon-info.net/stories/0,56764,@,cameroun-rca-apres-la-rca-laquo-la-france-a-des-plans-contingents-pour-le-camero.htmlConsulté le 09/02/2016 à 20h45
http://www.cotedivoire.news/actualite/8650-top-10-hommes-plus-riches-cameroun-2017.html. Consulté le 07/09/2017 à 20h45
https://www.voaafrique.com/a/les-30-plus-grosses-fortunes-d-afrique-francophone-pesent-10-milliards-de-dollars-selon-forbes-afrique/3620354.htmlConsulté le 07/09/2017 à 20h55

http://www.cotedivoire.news/actualite/8650-top-10-hommes-plus-riches-cameroun-2017.html. Consultéle 07/09/2017 à 21H

http://www.rfi.fr/afrique/20100714-1960-2010-50-ans-interventions-militaires-francaises-afrique Consulté le 29/01/2014 à 21h43

https://fr.sputniknews.com/infographies/20130403197984290/ Consulté le 11/02/2017 à 21h38

https://fr.wikipedia.org/wiki/Pr%C3%A9sidence_tournante Consulté le 11/02/2017 à 18h00

https://www.voaafrique.com/a/les-30-plus-grosses-fortunes-d-afrique-francophone-pesent-10-milliards-de-dollars-selon-forbes-afrique/3620354.htmlConsulté le du 07/09/2017

http://www.lemonde.fr/afrique/article/2017/10/09/au-cameroun-le-crepuscule-d-une-dictature-a-huis-clos_5198501_3212.html Consulté le 10/10/2017 à 18h09

http://www.faz.net/aktuell/politik/cdu-csu-merkel-plaediert-fuer-politik-der-mitte-124264.html Consulté le 12/10/2017 à 18h00

http://www.wathi.org/laboratoire/tribune/crise-gambienne-retrospective-juridique-lintervention-militaire-de-cedeao/ Consulté le 13/02/2016 à 11H10

https://en-marche.fr/ Consulté le 12/10/2017 à 19h06

http://www.lefigaro.fr/international/2017/10/19/01003-20171019ARTFIG00319-crise-catalane-les-europeens-font-bloc-pour-l-unite-de-l-espagne.php Consulté le 24/10/2017 à 13h27

https://en.wikipedia.org/wiki/G5_Sahel du 31/10/2017

http://www.foretiafoundation.org/wp-content/uploads/2017/07/Akere-Muna_THINGS-FALL-APART-min.pdf, consulté le 13/09/2017, p.3

https://www.reuters.com/article/us-ivorycoast-politics-ouattara/ivory-coasts-ouattara-says-hes-free-to-run-again-in-2020-jeune-afrique-idUSKCN1IZ0S3 consulted on June,6th 2018

# Appendixes

## Qui est le père de la rotation régionale du pouvoir ?

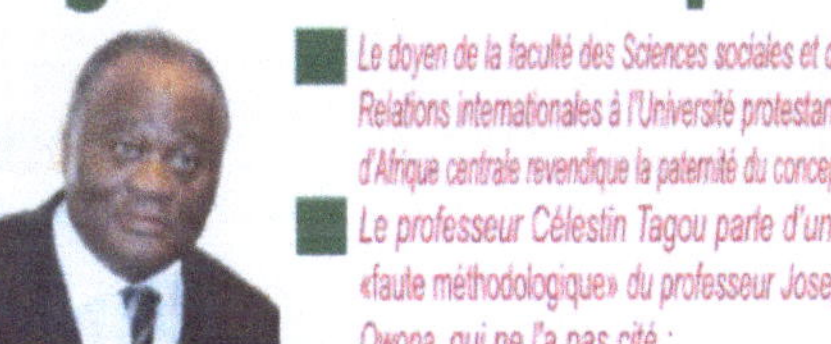

Le doyen de la faculté des Sciences sociales et des Relations internationales à l'Université protestante d'Afrique centrale revendique la paternité du concept ;

Le professeur Célestin Tagou parle d'une «faute méthodologique» du professeur Joseph Owona, qui ne l'a pas cité ;

Réaction de l'agrégé de droit public et de sciences politiques.

>>> P. 6

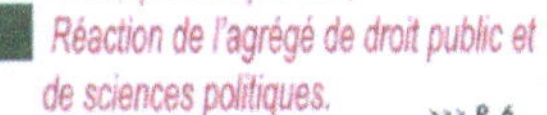

## CÉLESTIN TAGOU

# Mes travaux sont antérieurs à cette publication

L'universitaire parle du concept de la rotation du pouvoir suprême entre toutes les régions du pays. Idée évoquée par Joseph Owona dans son dernier ouvrage.

**Pourquoi revendiquez-vous la paternité du concept de la « rotation régionale » ou « rotation du pouvoir suprême entre les régions du Cameroun», idée évoquée par Joseph Owona dans son dernier ouvrage intitulé : « les systèmes politiques précoloniaux au Cameroun »?**

Je voudrais d'abord vous remercier pour l'intérêt que vous portez à ma modeste personne et à mes travaux scientifiques. Quand j'ai lu votre papier du 25 janvier dernier et par la suite les commentaires online d'autres organes de presse sur l'essentiel de l'ouvrage du Prof. Joseph Owona dont la dédicace a eu lieu le 22 janvier à l'Institut relations internationales du Cameroun (Iric), je me suis réjoui du fait qu'enfin un maître emboîte le pas aux pistes de solutions qui sont au centre de mes préoccupations épistémologiques et de mes démarches scientifiques depuis plus d'une décennie. Mais à la lecture de l'ouvrage en question, je me suis rendu compte que mes travaux sur la même approche ne figurent nulle part dans les références. Il était donc juste que le monde académique et l'opinion sachent que mes travaux scientifiques dans lesquels je propose cette solution pour les pays africains en général et plus précisément pour notre pays le Cameroun sont antérieurs à la publication du Prof. Joseph Owona. En effet, à la suite de mes recherches doctorales entre 2002 et 2006 à la Wolfgang Goethe-Universität Frankfurt am Main en République fédérale d'Allemagne, j'ai publié *Demokratisches Rotationsprinzip: Eine Lösungsapplikation Integration in Kamerun zwischen Nationalstaat und Ethnizität* en 2006 chez Cuvillier VerlagGöttingen, où le concept de la rotation du pouvoir suprême entre les régions au Cameroun a été largement présenté dans tous ses contours socio-politique, institutionnel, juridique et démocratique; en 2011, j'ai co-publié en tant que premier auteur, *Les limites du Power Sharing dans la gestion des conflits politiques et ethno-régionaux en Afrique : le cas de la Côte d'Ivoire* dans la *African Journal of Peace Communication and Development*, revue annuelle de la faculté des sciences sociales et relations internationales de l'université protestante d'Afrique centrale. Dans cet article de 2011, nous avons testé la transposabilité ou l'implémentation du modèle théorique de la démocratie rotative entre les régions en Côte d'Ivoire en lieu et place des outcomes des accords de paix d'Ouagadougou. Enfin et après deux communications à Trinity College à Washington DC et à Dakar, j'ai publié *Managing ethno-regionaldiversities in African states : Western peaceparadigms versusAfricanpeacephilosophy and a politicalway out* dans le 3e numéro de *Mapinduzi Journal* portant sur *Identity and governance in Africa* en 2013 à Berlin. A partir de la page 153 de cet article, j'actualise mon modèle théorique de la Démocratie Rotative entre les régions au Cameroun en tenant compte non seulement de la nouvelle donne sociopolitique et institutionnelle, mais aussi et surtout de l'évolution de l'esprit, du temps et du niveau de culture politique dans notre pays. Au vue donc de l'antériorité de mes travaux et de mes publications, je revendique la paternité intellectuelle et morale de l'idée de la rotation du pouvoir suprême entre les régions à la tête des États africains en proie aux irrédentismes et irréductibles replis ethno-régionaux.

**Concrètement s'agit-il d'un plagiat ?**

A la lecture de l'ouvrage du Prof. Joseph Owona, je ne parlerais pas de plagiat en mon âme et conscience, mais plus d'une faute méthodologique dans la démarche scientifique. Le professeur a sans doute eu la même idée que moi. Il lui a juste manqué le respect de la rigueur scientifique qui aurait voulu qu'il se rassente d'abord qu'aucun autre chercheur n'a pu énoncer et formuler l'idée avant lui. Ce n'est pas du plagiat parce que dans les deux premières parties, qui font d'ailleurs l'essentiel de l'analyse du prof. Joseph Owona, il fait une cartographie des systèmes d'organisation et de gestion sociopolitique des grands agrégats sociaux qu'a connu l'espace géographique devenu Kamerun, puis Cameroun et Cameroon et enfin République du Cameroun/Republic of Cameroon/dès différentes étapes de l'évolution historique et institutionnelle de notre pays. C'est dans sa conclusion que le professeur Joseph Owona, annonce de manière très brève l'idée de, je le cite : « une rotation du pouvoir suprême entre les régions du pays ... « comme « une des solutions d'avenir de mes institutions... ». C'est à ce niveau qu'il aurait dû me rendre justice, s'il avait pris un moment de fouille ne serait-ce que sur Internet, pour se rendre compte que j'ai formulé et analysé cette solution dans mes publications depuis 2006. Toutes nos publications mentionnées plus haut se trouvent non seulement dans plusieurs bibliothèques universitaires en Europe et sur les sites de mes éditeurs, mais aussi dans amazon.de, amazon.co.uk, amazon.fr, amazon.es, amazon.it, sur chez.de, books.google, etc...

Donc je pense que le professeur ne m'a pas cité tout simplement parce qu'il n'a pas eu l'occasion de lire mes travaux. Il n'est d'ailleurs pas le premier. Il y a un étudiant de la République démocratique du Congo qui a eu la même idée en 2010 dans son mémoire de master et a commis la maladresse de mettre son travail en vente numérique sur memoireonline. Mon éditeur de 2006, Cuvillier Verlag, est actuellement à leur trousse pour qu'il retire cela de leur site.

**A quoi renvoie précisément ce concept ?**

Avant de répondre à votre question, je tiens à dire qu'après la version allemande sous forme de livre en 2006 et les actualisations sous forme d'articles et de communications en Anglais et en Français entre 2009 et 2013, je travaille depuis 2014 sur une version française sous forme de livre dont le titre provisoire est : *Réinventer la gestion internationale des conflits en Afrique à partir des réalités endogènes : De la démocratie rotative en Côte d'Ivoire et au Cameroun*. Ici je vais d'abord procéder à une déconstruction des concepts de lignalogie, clan, tribu, ethnie, peuple, nation et État dans leur connotation au 18e et 19e siècle, et puis à une reconstruction de leur compréhension au 21e siècle avant de présenter l'architecture théorique et pratique de la démocratie rotative sur les deux cas d'études mentionnés.

Le concept de la démocratie rotative renvoie à un modèle d'organisation du processus d'accession à la magistrature suprême, dans notre cas à la présidence de la République. C'est un modèle encore théorique qui permettrait à un État dans un contexte pluriel, de transcender positivement et de transformer productivement la diversité ethno-régionale du peuple qui le constitue, en une nouvelle donne politique où la peur des uns de perdre le pouvoir pour toujours dans une réelle démocratie libérale et les frustrations des autres d'être à jamais relégués à la périphérie du pouvoir suprême, céderont la place à une acceptation politique mutuelle des uns et des autres, signe d'une intégration amalgamée à la Deutsch, mais surtout garantit des alternances politiques paisibles et démocratiques au sens simpliste de gouvernement du peuple par le peuple et pour le peuple. Vous comprenez que chez moi, la variable parti politique joue un rôle très important dans le modèle de la démocratie rotation.

**Selon votre approche de la démocratie rotative au Cameroun, seules quatre régions sur 10 sont concernées. Pourquoi ?**

Les autres variables fondamentales du modèle de la démocratie rotative sont ce que le groupe de l'Institute fürAfrikaKunde à Hambourg a appelé «strategischeGruppen» c'est-à-dire groupes stratégiques et «KonfliktsfähigeGruppen», autrement dit groupes conflictuels ou conflictogènes pour reprendre le Prof. Alain Didier Olinga. Ayant identifié ces groupes stratégiques et conflictuels dans un pays donné, on repère leur homeland ou leur régions d'origine. Dans le cas du Cameroun, je récuse les thèses de 150, 230 ou 250 langues qui équivaudraient à autant de groupe ethniques. Le faire c'est tomber dans le piège de ce que Théophile Obenga appelle à juste titre l'ethnologie coloniale, qui voudrait montrer aux Africains qu'ils sont trop différents les uns des autres et que le vivre ensemble serait très compliqué dans cette multitude de diversité. Me basant donc sur les thèses de Théophile Obenga et de son mentor Cheikh AntaDiop et faisant recours à Ferdinand de Saussure, à Frédéric Barth et à bien d'autres, je ne distingue dans notre pays qu'environ 7+1 groupes stratégiques et conflictuels. Donc quand je parle de région dans mes travaux, je ne renvoie pas à sa connotation administrative actuelle, où la Constitution de 1996 a réorganisé le découpage du pays en 10 régions administratives. Il s'agit chez moi de quatre régions dont le regroupement s'est fait sur la base des affinités historiques, culturelles et sociolinguistiques entre les 7+1 groupes, selon qu'on soit constructiviste ou essentialiste dans l'approche épistémologique en ethnologie ou en anthropologie. Les 10 régions administratives restent.

**Pensez-vous donc qu'un tel système puisse fonctionner dans un pays comme le Cameroun balkanisé et retranché derrière des barrières qui épousent l'actuel découpage administratif ?**

Ce n'est pas un système, mais un modèle théorique de réglementation et de régulation de l'accès au pouvoir suprême dans un pays donné, marqué par la pluralité et la diversité de son peuple. Bien évidemment que cela peut bien marcher dans notre pays. C'est d'ailleurs et en premier lieu pour notre pays que j'ai conçu ce modèle en 2006 et qui m'a valu un prix, sous forme de prise en charge des frais de publication, de la *Wilhelm-Hahn-undErben-Fondation* qui regroupe les donateurs de la Wolfgang Goethe-Universität Frankfurt am Main en République fédérale d'Allemagne.

Ce n'est pas dans le cadre d'une interview à un quotidien qu'on peut mieux expliquer dans ses détails les tenants et les aboutissants théoriques et pratiques, ainsi que les modalités institutionnelles et juridiques d'un tel modèle. La version française de mon livre annoncée plus haut apportera plus de précisions sur le pourquoi, le comment et les instruments de la démocratie rotative. Un modèle qui se veut être non seulement un arsenal de réglementations pour un accès au pouvoir suprême de manière paisible, en garantissant les alternances politiques dans un contexte pluriel comme le nôtre, mais surtout comme une riposte à la panacée passe-par-tout que Timothy Sisk, Donald Rotschild et les autres ont vendu à la communauté internationale pour résoudre les conflits ethno-régionaux sur notre continent : le Power Sharing. Un partage de pouvoir dont le outcome reste en définitive un Win/Lose eurocentrique qui se révèle dans le séduisme de la paix négative. La démocratie rotative débouche sur le Win/Win, c'est la paix positive, c'est la transcendance positive selon Johan Galtung et c'est africain. Et comme j'ai indiqué en 2013 *« this model is... worth a try »*, car les instruments sont développés ; reste maintenant le degré de transcendance des acteurs du jeu politique !

*PROPOS RECUEILLIS PAR*
*YANICK YEMGA*

## Réaction de Joseph Owona

■ Je n'ai jamais lu ce monsieur. Si je l'avais lu, je l'aurais cité, comme je l'ai fait pour tous ceux qui ont travaillé dans ce champ d'étude. Peut-être, il a réalisé des travaux qui ne sont pas de réputation publique. Avez-vous lu ses travaux? Moi, honnêtement, je n'en ai pas connaissance.